Read and Write A

Read and Write Arabic Script

Mourad Diouri

Hodder Education
338 Euston Road, London NW1 3BH.

Hodder Education is an Hachette UK company

First published in UK 2011 by Hodder Education

The publisher has used its best endeavours to ensure that any
website addresses referred to in this book are correct and active at
the time of going to press. However, the publisher and the author
have no responsibility for the websites and can make no guarantee
that a site will remain live or that the content will remain relevant,
decent or appropriate.

The publisher has made every effort to mark as such all words which
it believes to be trademarks. The publisher should also like to make
it clear that the presence of a word in the book, whether marked or
unmarked, in no way affects its legal status as a trademark.

Every reasonable effort has been made by the publisher to trace the
copyright holders of material in this book. Any errors or omissions
should be notified in writing to the publisher, who will endeavour to
rectify the situation for any reprints and future editions.

Hachette UK's policy is to use papers that are natural, renewable
and recyclable products and made from wood grown in sustainable
forests. The logging and manufacturing processes are expected to
conform to the environmental regulations of the country of origin.

www.hoddereducation.co.uk

Typeset by Cenveo Publisher Services.

Printed and bound by CPI Group (UK) Ltd, Croydon CR0 4YY.

Contents

Dedication

*This is the first book I have ever written,
dedicated to my first love and cherished wife.*

Umm-Taha

أم طه

Meet the author

Mourad Diouri, currently an eLearning lecturer and developer
in Arabic language studies at the University of Edinburgh, is of
Moroccan origin. He has spent almost a decade of his professional
career teaching languages at numerous institutions across the UK.

His career and passion for teaching began at the University of East
Anglia. While there he won the University's Teaching Award for
the 'Most Innovative Course Design' for 2005. He then moved
to Edinburgh to take up his current post, where his passion for
language was combined with his interest in technology. Now
specializing in TELL (Technology Enhanced Language Learning),
Mourad made it his personal mission to modernize and advance
the teaching of Arabic and other foreign languages. As a result, he
was shortlisted for an eLearning Award in 2009.

His dual expertise and renowned creativity have crystallized in this
book, making the learning of Arabic not only an attainable skill
but also a skill that can be put into practice in real life.

In his teaching, Mourad has always adopted the view that
language can be picked up more effectively with visual and
auditory immersion in authentic language using a wide variety
of resources, in particular real-life items that reflect the target
language and culture.

In a continuous effort to support learners and teachers of Arabic
worldwide and online, he has developed and continues to update
two well-known portals:

e-Arabic learners' portal at www.e-Arabic.com
e-Arabic teachers' portal at www.v-Arabic.com

Only got a minute?

أَ هْلاً وَسَهْلاً وَمَرْحَباً !

ahlan wa sahlan wa marhaban
Welcome to 'Read and Write Arabic Script'!

At first glance, the Arabic script could seem impenetrable, especially when the only letters you've been familiar with are Latin-based, as they are in English. However, you will be pleased to know that Arabic is, in fact, a fascinating, logical and easy language to read and write. It has only 28 letters in its alphabet – *al-hamdu lilaah* الحَمْدُ لله ('thanks to God') – and you are required in this book to learn only around ten core shapes or family letters to master the entire script. You will also be delighted to know that learning to read and write the Arabic alphabet will grant you access not just to one, but to many languages whose writing systems Arabic has influenced profoundly. Today, non-Arab countries such as Afghanistan, China, India, Iran, Pakistan and Israel use the Arabic script in one or more of their national languages and amongst the many languages written in Arabic – with a few modifications – are Dari (spoken in Afghanistan), Kashmiri, Kurdish, Malay, Persian, Punjabi, Pashto (Afghanistan), Urdu and Sindhi (Pakistan).

More good news to reassure you is the fact that you 'already speak Arabic' in one way or another! There are thousands of Arabic loanwords in the European languages, not only in the fields of mathematics (e.g. *algebra*, *algorithm*), chemistry (e.g. *alchemy*) and astronomy, but also in commonly used vocabulary adopted in the Middle Ages, such as *sugar, magazine, coffee, zero, average and hazard*.

The Arabic script can be written in a wide variety of creative styles ranging from simple handwriting to artistic calligraphy, all written cursively with astonishing beauty and elegance.

I have no doubt that you will find learning the script an enjoyable and satisfying experience.

5 Only got five minutes?

Arabic in a nutshell

Although it is often regarded as mysterious and inaccessible, Arabic
(العربية) /al-ᶜarabiyya/ is an easy language to learn and understand.
It has a regular spelling system that is much less confusing than
English and it has a consistent pronunciation of sounds. To give
you an example, can you think of how many ways the letter "s" is
pronounced in English?

To get you started, read these words paying attention to the
phonetics of the letter "s": s̲ugar, vis̲ual, cars̲, s̲cene, s̲on, is̲land.

In Arabic, every different sound of "s" in this list corresponds to a
unique and different letter.[1]

Because of the phonetic consistency of the language, when you try
to learn the pronunciation of Arabic sounds, Arabs can confidently
claim: "What you hear is what you write!"

Nevertheless, it is true that there are some sounds in Arabic that
are unfamiliar to the Western ear and can be tricky to sound out,
but with persistent practice and attentive listening you will learn
them in no time.

Arabic is one of the world's major languages. It ranks high in the
world's league table of languages as it has gained an international
reputation as the sixth language spoken in the UN since 1973. It
is currently the official language of 26 countries, the fifth most
spoken after Mandarin Chinese, Hindi/Urdu, Spanish and English.
Arabic is part of the Semitic linguistic family, which includes
Hebrew, Aramaic and others.

---

[1] /sh/ in sugar, /j/ in visual, /z/ in cars, /s/ in scene, an emphatic /s/ in son and a silent /s/ in island.

It is widely spoken by approximately 300 million speakers across the Arab world, comprising North African countries from the shores of Morocco, the Fertile Crescent of the Middle East, Arab peninsula and the Gulf states. This is in addition to the majority of non-Arab speaking Muslims around the world who can read Arabic with varying fluency for religious purposes. Non-native Arabic speakers from the Muslim world are located mainly in Indonesia (the largest Muslim country by population), Bangladesh, Pakistan and India.

The Qur'an (القرآن) /al-qur'ān/ (lit. the recital) is one of the earliest surviving documents of written Arabic and is considered by Muslims as the book of divine guidance and the final revelation of *Allah* (God) for mankind. Arabic is regarded as a universal language for Muslims worldwide and considered as the liturgical language of Islam.

Arabic has always been the linguistic vehicle by which Islam was introduced as a new way of life. In fact, the influence of Arabic is considered as pervasive due the highly language-specific nature of Islam (Versteegh, 2001).

Muslims, who comprise around one-fifth of the world's population, use Arabic on a daily basis in prayers, greetings, and supplications. Likewise, it is an essential key to understand and appreciate the teaching of the Qur'an and that of the prophet of Islam, Muhammad.

Other languages written in Arabic

Other than Arabic, there are many non-Semitic languages that have adopted – and adapted – the Arabic script for use in their writing system. Among the commonly known languages written in the Arabic script with adaptations are Persian, Urdu, Kurdish, Sindhi, Uighur and some Berber languages in North Africa.

While these languages continue to use the Arabic script, nowadays other languages, which were previously written in Arabic, have been replaced with a different script, for example, Turkish, Swahili,

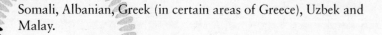

Somali, Albanian, Greek (in certain areas of Greece), Uzbek and Malay.

THE IMPACT OF ARABIC ON EUROPEAN LANGUAGES

With the wide spread of Islam throughout Western Europe and its linguistic domination throughout the Middle Ages, Arabic was regarded as the lingua franca and the "Latin" language of scholarship, literature, science and trade, not only in Europe but across the world for nearly a century of its existence in the Iberian peninsula.

In his book *"Europe speaks Arabic"*, Rahim summarized the impact of Arabic on European language eloquently:

> Arabic gave Europe cotton to wear, candy to eat, coffee to drink, chess to play, magazine to read, sofa to recline on, mattress to sleep on, cipher to calculate with, cable to communicate with, racket to play tennis with, sugar to sweeten with, cheque to draw money with, and a host of other words.

You might be surprised to know that you already speak some Arabic! Most non-Arab speakers can probably recognize obvious Arabic loanwords, such as algebra, algorithm, alchemy, camel, sahara and zenith, and needless to say the names of famous Arab dishes, including couscous, falafel, hummus, halwa, baklava and many others.

But you may not know that the following day-to-day words are originally Arabic: alcohol; atlas; average; camera; candy; coffee; cheque; guitar; hazard; magazine; mask; mattress; racket; soda; sofa; sugar; syrup; zero and many more!

Arabic, like many other languages, has the capacity to absorb and accommodate other languages and vice versa. It is well established as a major source for vocabulary for many languages it has come into direct contact with. Some are European, predominately Spanish, Portuguese, Maltese and Cypriot Greek, while others are mainly Eastern such as Persian, Urdu, Bengali, Turkish, Malay and Indonesian. As a result, Arabic has left a long-lasting impact on these languages, their vocabulary and even some of their grammatical structures.

Spanish language has absorbed by far the largest proportion of words – around 4000 – due to its direct contact with Islamic civilisation. Words such as aduana (customs), aceite (oil), aceituna (olives), albaricoque (apricot), almohada (pillow), ojalá (may God will it) and many more are not unintelligible to a native Arab speaker.

English, by way of contrast, has around 3000 loanwords (in addition to 5000 derivatives). Throughout Units 1–10, you will be introduced gradually to many frequently used English words of Arabic origin.

One language, many dialects

The Arabic language is enriched with a large variety of spoken dialects known collectively as colloquial Arabic.

Arabic is of three types: classical, modern standard and colloquial:

1 **Classical/Qur'anic Arabic** is the language of the Qur'an القُرآن, the poetry of pre-Islamic Arabia and the classical literature of the Golden Age of Islam.
2 **Modern Standard/literary Arabic**, known as al-fuṣḥā الفُصْحى (the pure), is the descendant of classical Arabic. It is the literary language used, both spoken and written, in the contemporary Arab world, mainly in the media, printed publications and in formal speeches. It is understood and used by educated Arab speakers depending on the degree of formality and the situation.
3 **Colloquial/Dialectal Arabic**, known as Dārija الدّارِجَة, is the universal means of informal everyday conversation among Arabs and in spoken media (e.g. talk shows and soap operas). Many national and regional varieties of dialects exist.

The complexity and the co-existence of two varieties, colloquial (spoken) and literary Arabic (mostly written), within one single language is referred to as the sociolinguistic phenomenon of diglossia, which makes every Arab bilingual by default. The major dialect groups are Egyptian, Maghrebi, Iraqi, Gulf and Levantine Arabic.

Arabic sounds and vowels

At first, Arabic with its unique and distinct sounds might come across as unpronounceable and intimidating to the foreign ear, especially sounds that have no equivalent in European languages. However, with diligent practice and careful listening, anyone can master these sounds. Arabic is enriched with numerous pronunciation and vocalisation markers and symbols. These are normally omitted in most writings except in children's books, the Qur'an and elementary schoolbooks. There are three short vowels /a/, /i/, /u/ in the form of diacritics, three alphabetical long vowels /ā/, /ī/, /ū/, and further supplementary vowels (see Arabic vowels and pronunciation symbols).

Arabic numerals

Numbers, referred to as Arabic numerals and used throughout the world, originated in India and were then adopted and modified by Arabs. These numerals were the founding blocks of modern mathematics in Europe following the invention of algebra, algorithm and trigonometry by Arab mathematicians. Indian numerals are used widely in the Gulf and misconceived as Arabic. The concept of sifr (zero) is another contribution of the Arabs and led to words such as cipher and the french *chiffre* (see Appendices).

Introduction

To dispel the prejudice that Arabic is impenetrable, complicated and hard to learn, this book will give you a comprehensive idea about how the written system works and how to master reading and writing the script, both printed and handwritten. Whilst learning to master the script, you will simultaneously acquire basic and commonly-used vocabulary, which will be useful for further progression to the next level. You will also be acquainted with vital facts and figures about the Arabic language and script. Fascinating areas of the Arabic script will be covered, namely calligraphy, script styles and designs, transcription of foreign words and additional, less commonly known letters.

As the series title 'Teach Yourself' suggests, the book is designed for independent self-study, but it can also be used as a resource from which to teach in a classroom setting. To make the book more interactive, the author offers readers ample opportunities to practise the skills acquired and to read and recognize the script via many visual and eye-catching illustrations in a variety of real-life contexts – something that distinguishes this book from many others.

By the end, you will have achieved a level of proficiency in script recognition, reading and writing, which will allow you to easily read the variety of scripts found in newspapers, public signs, calligraphy and handwriting. Understanding the content of the written material will require further study beyond recognition level.

How to use this book

This book is specifically written for an English-speaking audience with no previous knowledge of the Arabic script. It is a beginners' reference to the Arabic script, its writing systems and a wide selection of essential vocabulary. The script will be presented in bite-sized small groups of letters, and you will be introduced to the alphabet letters in a gradual and step-by-step way, rather than being taught the entire alphabet at once.

The main emphasis of this book is on reading and writing the script in its numerous varieties and styles, hand-written and printed. Also, you will learn a wide range of useful and basic vocabulary as well as some basic grammar rules which will be essential for you to learn before embarking on further study.

Practical and basic vocabulary will be introduced primarily as examples to teach you the script whilst simultaneously building your Arabic wordpower. All the vocabulary is listed by theme in the Appendices section. Easy basic grammar points will also be highlighted during the teaching of the script, but grammar is not the main emphasis of this book which is, after all, about the script.

Each of the core Units contains:

- a list of the letters to be learnt;
- how to read them;
- a chance to use them in real contexts.

Then at the end of each of these Units, you will find:

- **Insights** which provide fascinating further information about the script.
- **Summary** of the most important points in the Unit.
- **Arabic quotation:** Arabic is rich in proverbs and wisdoms, which are part of everyday spoken and written Arabic dialogue and literature. To expose you to the poetic nature and cultural wealth of Arabic you will be rewarded at the end of each lesson with a selected famous saying, beautiful both in language and meaning. It will be selected not only to help you practise your reading of the script but also to introduce you to the wisdom of the Arabs and how this authentically reflects the way many Arabs live and communicate. The quotations will be displayed in a variety of calligraphic styles. You are strongly advised to read aloud and memorize these quotations to enhance your spoken Arabic.
- **Test yourself section** to consolidate your reading and writing practice.

To help you check your progress, answers to the exercises are provided at the end of the book.

ABBREVIATIONS

ة/	feminine tā'
pl.	plural
m.	masculine
f.	feminine
coll.	colloquial
lit.	literally
MSA	Modern Standard Arabic

How to read and write Arabic: essential hints and tips

Learning the Arabic script is a gradual learning process. Learn it in stages.

Below are useful tips and hints to help you master reading and writing the script fluently.

1 Practise, practise, practise! As with learning any language, the mastery of writing the script comes with persistence, perseverance and lots of practise. The more you practise, the more fluent you will become. Arabs have a witty proverb they use when they wish to emphasize the value of practise: التكرار يعلم الشطار /a(l)t-tikrār youᶜallim a(l)sh-shaṭār/ 'Practise teaches even the intelligent.'

2 **First things first:** In order to be able to read Arabic correctly, you should focus on learning the different vowels and pronunciation signs before you start learning the consonants. Once you master these, you will be able to read and decipher the Arabic script more easily and accurately.

3 **Focus on the core shapes:** First, familiarize yourself with the basic skeleton shapes of the script. There are only ten basic shapes to learn. Furthermore, learn to recognize individual letters in isolation before attempting to join them up.

4 **One letter group at a time:** Don't try to learn the whole alphabet at once. The smart way is to group them together by their basic skeleton shape. When you start studying the letters in groups, you will notice how each group contains 2–5 letters that share the exact basic skeleton. However, the main differences to bear in mind are the number of dots (1 or 2) and/or their position (above or below the letter).

5 **Take it in stages:** First, write out the main skeleton shape of a letter, then add any distinguishing dots. Write it out several

times in the standalone form. Then write the letter out in its different forms and observe the changes it undergoes in each different position. Read out loud while you write. Connect the three forms together in a cursive style to form an imaginary word. Learn to write the script joined up with other letters to form meaningful Arabic words.

6 **Write it down:** Make a habit of carrying a small notebook with you to practise writing and recording new vocabulary as you learn it. Arabs like to stress this advice in their saying: قيدوا العلم بالكتابة /qayyidū al-ᶜilm bi al-kitābah/ 'Inscribe knowledge with writing.'

7 **One step at a time:** Since learning script is progressive, don't rush yourself by skipping units. The units are designed to be learned in sequence and build upon each other. Pace yourself by consolidating what you have learnt before moving onto the next lesson. Also, try to complete the tests before checking the answers!

8 **Immerse yourself in Arabic:** go beyond learning the script in this book and expose yourself to authentic written and spoken Arabic in real contexts. In the virtual world, you may visit Arabic news sites, watch live TV online or listen to live radio. In the real world, you may wish to explore a variety of items (e.g. shop and road signs, currency notes, children books, etc.) available at your local Arabic supermarkets, restaurants or bookshops. Whenever you come across Arabic writing, make every effort to decipher it. If possible, write it down or, much better, take a photo of it and practise writing it out at home.

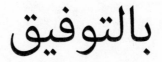

بالتوفيق

/bit-tawfīq/

Good luck

Arabic transliteration and pronunciation guide

This section deals with the different ways of pronouncing Arabic sounds correctly and how to transliterate or romanize Arabic script into Latin script.

Arabic transliteration or romanisation is a method of attempting to give an idea of the sound of Arabic utterances using the Latin alphabet. There are various systems of transliteration and transcription in use depending on the degree of accuracy required. Obviously a linguist will strive for greater accuracy than someone texting a friend or an author spicing his English novel with a few Arabic names and expressions. To learn how to transcribe foreign words into Arabic, see Unit 11.

Although proper pronunciation of Arabic is crucial to your learning and mastery of the language, it is arguably very difficult to teach yourself authentic pronunciation using only transliteration.

In fact, one of the best ways to master pronunciation of any language, but particularly Arabic, is attentive and regular listening to authentic Arabic speech from real-life conversations by native speakers, audio-visual media or recorded audio learning material.

Care must be taken when you pronounce new words because if an Arabic word is pronounced incorrectly, you run the risk of communicating a different meaning e.g. /kul/ (eat!) is not the same as /qul/ (say!) and /qalbi/ (my heart) is certainly different from /kalbi/ (my dog)!

A variety of phonetic transliteration symbols and letters have been adopted by different individuals and organisations to show you how the words should sound. However, it is not always practical to show exactly in writing how to pronounce words, especially if the sounds do not have an English equivalent.

Bear in mind that these symbols show you how the word is pronounced phonetically and not how it is spelled (e.g. "sun" is written as الشَّمْس "al-shams" but pronounced as "ash-shams" with a silent "l" and double "sh").

Ideally, if you wish to attain good pronunciation of Modern Standard Arabic or a particular regional dialect, it is recommended that you listen to a native or near-native Arabic speaker. Listening to audio learning resources and authentic media is immensely useful in improving your pronunciation of Arabic sounds.

You will be pleased to know that, unlike English, Arabic is phonetically a consistent language. For instance, learners of English have to learn five different irregular phonetic sounds of the letter "s", where there is only one distinct Arabic letter for each of the five sounds.

English sound	Pronunciation	Arabic equivalent
seen	frontal "s"	س
son	emphatic and deep "s"	ص
sugar	normal frontal "sh"	ش
visual	j (in courgette)	ج
cars	z (in zoo)	ز

Some Arabic sounds are unique to Arabic whereas others have equivalents or approximate sounds in English and other European languages. Phonetic sounds are classified as:

- **emphatic:** pronounced deep and from the back of the throat;
- **non-emphatic:** pronounced from the front of the mouth.

The following table lists all the Arabic letters and sounds with their approximate equivalents.

Arabic letter	Phonetic transliteration	Approximate equivalent sound	Further explanation
ا / أ	aa or ā (vowel) ' (consonant)	father (vowel) at (consonant)	p. xxxiv (vowel) pp. 4 and 6 (consonant)
ب	b	boat	pp. 21–22
ت	t	tea	p. 24
ث	th	three	p. 27
ج	j	jam, game or visual	pp. 101–102
ح	h̲	hot, voiceless and breathy "h"	p. 105
خ	kh	close to Scottish "lo<u>ch</u>"	pp. 111–112
د	d	dice	p. 74
ذ	dh	though	p. 76
ر	r	roll	pp. 84–88
ز	z	zoo	pp. 87–88
س	s	sea	pp. 121–122
ش	sh	sheep	pp. 128–129
ص	s̲	close to "sore", emphatic counterpart of Sīn س	p. 141
ض	d̲	close to "<u>d</u>onkey" or "<u>d</u>oll" emphatic counterpart of Dāl د	pp. 144–145
ط	t̲	no equivalent, emphatic counterpart of Tā' ت	p. 149
ظ	dh̲	no equivalent, emphatic counterpart of Dhāl ذ	p. 153

ع	ʿ	no equivalent	pp. 164–165
غ	gh	no equivalent, close to French "Pa<u>r</u>is" voiced counterpart of Khā	p. 171
ف	f	five	pp. 179–180
ق	q	no equivalent, emphatic counterpart of Kāf ك	pp. 182–183
ك	k	kayak	p. 62
ل	l	lamb	p. 8
م	m	mime	p. 46
ن	n	nine	p. 30
ه	h	no equivalent, voiced counterpart of Hā ح	p. 53
و	ū (vowel) w (consonant)	m<u>oo</u>n wow	p. xxxv (vowel) p. 91 (consonant)
ي	ii or ī (vowel) y (consonant)	b<u>ee</u> (vowel) York (consonant)	p. xxxvi (vowel) p. 34 (consonant)

Although transliteration is a useful method for beginners learning Arabic *ab initio*, it should be only a temporary solution to writing the script and it is always recommended to write Arabic in its original script. Indeed, when learners rely mainly on transliteration instead of the actual Arabic script, it becomes an obstacle to learning rather than an aid.

In fact, once you master the writing system, you should accustom yourself to writing solely in Arabic.

Arabic script and computers

Typing the Arabic script on the computer has never been easier and more accessible than it is today. Initially, most text communication technologies such as email, IM (instant messaging) and text messaging were originally designed for Latin-based communication with minimal support for Arabic characters. As a result, Arabic-speaking computer users used to – and some even continue to – communicate by transliterating Arabic into Latin script. This practice led to a new type of writing known as Arabizi, Arabish (Arabic chat alphabet) or IM Arabic.

For certain Arabic letters, similar looking or sounding letters, numerals and other characters are adopted and vary from author to author, as the following table shows.

Arabic letter	Transliteration character	Example
ᶜayn ع	3 (reverse of ع) or superscript c (ᶜ)	al-3arabiyya (Arabic)
Hā' ح	7	Mar7aban (welcome)
Hamza ء	2	Masaa2 (evening)
Dhā' ظ	6'	6'uhr (noon)
Dād ض	D	bayDa (egg)

The following screenshots display more transliteration shortcuts and characters adopted by two well-known online transliteration tools, Yamli™ and eiktub™.

Just over a few years, a wide variety of online real-time transliteration tools has emerged to support using Arabic script online and allow users to type Arabic without an Arabic keyboard using any Latin-based keyboard. Among the latest are Yamli™, eiktub™, Google Ta3reeb™ and Microsoft Maren™.

search the Arabic web.
use an English keyboard.

write Arabic using English letters as you hear it. Tips will appear here to help you out.

- Hide character map   Google search   Example: Al-e3laan

	ô	ổ	ẻ	ẻ	ﺫ	ﺵ	ﺹ	ﺽ	ﻁ	ﻅ	ع	ﻍ
A	t'	c	H	K	z'	x	S	D	T	Z	E	w	y
	h'	th	kh	dh	sh							
				7	5			9	9'	6	6'	3
	ا	و	ى	ﺱ	ﺇ	ا	ﺇ	ﻍ	ﺓ	ﺀ	ال التعريف
aa	ui oo	ii	aaa	i	l	i	ĝ	e	e, 2, '	Al-

Type it the way you say it.

You can also use these optional shortcuts
(case sensitive).

ع	3	ق	Q/8/9	ا	aa/A
ء	2	ك	K	و	oo/w
ح	7/H	ﻁ	T/6	ي	y/ee
خ	5/7'/kh	ظ	Z/6'	ذ	DH/dh
غ	gh/gu/3'	ص	S/9	ث	TH/th
		ﺽ	D/9'		

You can also use a dash ("-") to group words
together.
Example:
kal-aghani → كالأغاني

For more help, try our tutorial.

Google has also developed a vocalization tool (Google Tashkeel™.),
which adds missing diacritics or vowel signs to unvocalized Arabic
text.

Arabic script and alphabet

Although, at first sight, the Arabic script seems quite intimidating and somehow daunting to unravel, in fact, it is much easier to read and write than it looks!

Facts and figures about the Arabic script

The Arabic script is one of the world's major writing forms. After the Latin alphabet, it is the second most widely used alphabet around the world and it has been adopted by several languages around the world such as Persian, Kurdish, Malay and Urdu.

MAIN FEATURES OF THE ARABIC SCRIPT

- **Arabic is written and read from right to left.** Arabic publications (e.g. newspapers, magazines, books) open and are read at the opposite end of the ones you find in the Western world. When you study Arabic, try to "switch" your thinking, writing and reading from left to right!

Reading direction ⟵ تَحْتَوِي الْعَرَبِيَّة عَلَى 28 حَرْفاً مَكْتُوباً. وَيَرَى بَعْضُ اللُّغَوِيِّينَ أَنَّهُ يَجِبُ إِضَافَةُ حَرْفِ الهَمْزَةِ إِلَى حُرُوفِ العَرَبِيَّةِ، لِيُصْبِحَ عَدَدُ الْحُرُوفِ 29. تُكْتَبُ الْعَرَبِيَّةُ مِنَ البَمِينِ إِلَى اليَسَارِ - مِثْلُهَا اللُّغَة الْفَارِسِيَّة وَالْعِبْرِيَّة وَعَلَى عَكْسِ الكَثِيْرِ مِنَ اللُّغَاتِ العَالَمِيَّةِ...

- **There are 28 letters in total in the alphabet.** However, the good news is that for the sake of simplifying your learning of the script and to make it an easy and enjoyable experience, we are going to group the letters together into groups of two to five letters based on their common features and skeleton shape. As a result, you will only have to learn ten basic shapes instead of 28, as it is traditionally taught! From these main shapes, around two or three letters can be derived from them and the apparent differences between these letters are the number of dots they carry, their position and, of course, the way they are pronounced or additional minor features. From the core shapes, we obtain 28 letters, i.e. the whole alphabet.

- **There are no capital or lowercase letters in Arabic.**
- **The script is cursive by nature.** Most of the letters are joined up together both in handwriting and print, with varieties in style. This feature allows Arabic to be written in a variety of spectacular and breathtaking calligraphic works of art (see Unit 15).

Cursive Arabic script (the letters are unconnected):

←المَرْءُ مِنْ حَيْثُ يَثْبُت لا مِنْ حَيْثُ يَنْتُب   وَمِنْ حَيْثُ يوجَدُ لا مِنْ حَيْثُ يولَد

Non-cursive Arabic script (this is how the same text looks if the script is not connected):

ا ل مَ رْ ءُ مِ نْ حَ يْ ثُ يَ ثْ بُ ت لا مِ نْ حَ يْـ ثُ يَ نْ تُ ب

وَ مِ نْ حَ يْ   ثُ يو جَ دُ لا مِ نْ حَ يْ ثُ يو لَ د

Out of 28 connecting letters, there are six that never join the following one to the left. They are called "non-connecting" letters (see Units 4 and 6):

←ا د ذ ر ز و

- **Arabic letters change shape with their position in a word.** In writing the script, each letter has four written shapes (with the exception of the six non-connecting letters) that all share the core form and depend on their position in the word (isolated, initial, middle and final). Most letters have similar shaped 'tails' that are assimilated into the cursive writing according to their position in the word (initial, medial or final).
- **Arabic script has two levels of script writing.** Vowels are indicated with optional symbols. In addition to alphabet letters, there are supplementary non-alphabetical letters and symbols:

    The first layer (main skeleton of the word) is made up of consonants and long vowels.

The second layer (vocalisation markings) consists of short vowels, pronunciation markers and other grammatical endings. This second layer is normally omitted in most writings except in elementary schoolbooks, classical literary texts, religious texts (e.g. Qur'an) and unknown or difficult words.

تَحْتَوِي الْعَرَبِيَّةَ عَلَى 28 حَرْفاً مَكْتُوباً. وَيَرَى بَعْضُ اللُّغَوِيِّنَ أَنَّهُ يَجِبُ إِضَافَةُ حَرْفِ الهَمْزَةِ. إِلَىَ حُرُوفِ العَرَبِيَّةِ، لِيُصْبِحَ عَدَدُ الْحُرُوفَ 29

تحتوي العربية على 28 حرفًا مكتوبًا. ويرى بعض اللغويين أنه يجب إضافة حرف الهمزة. إلى حروف العربية، ليصبح عدد الحروف 29

JOINING UP LETTERS: GENERAL RULES

Due to the cursive nature of letters, most of the consonants can be joined up from both sides and hence will be written in four slightly different shapes:

- **The isolated form** is written:
    when the letters are in isolation (e.g. abbreviation, numerical letter);
    at the end of a word when preceded by, but not connected to, one of the six non-connecting letters.
- **The initial form** is written when:
    the letters are at the beginning of a word;
    the letters lose their tail and connect to the following letter to the left.
- **The middle form** is written when:
    the letters are located in the middle of a word;
    the letters are connected on both sides.

Note: Sometimes, the letter could be in the middle position but have the shape of an initial form. This is because, when the six non-connecting letters precede any letter, they cannot join them, hence the initial form is used.

- **The final form** is written when:
    the letters are positioned at the end of a word;
    the letters are connected to a letter to the right.

Arabic alphabet in dictionary order

Transli-teration	Joined up in one word	Final form	Medial form	Initial form	Name	Script: isolated form
ā	١١١*	ـا	ـا	ا	Alif	أَلِف ا
b	ببب	ـب	ـبـ	بـ	Bā	باء ب
t	تتت	ـت	ـتـ	تـ	Tā	تاء ت
th	ثثث	ـث	ـثـ	ثـ	Thā'	ثاء ث
j	ججج	ـج	ـجـ	جـ	Jeem	جيم ج
ḥ	ححح	ـح	ـحـ	حـ	Ḥā'	حاء ح
kh	خخخ	ـخ	ـخـ	خـ	Khā'	خاء خ
d	د د د*	ـد	ـد	د	Dāl	دال د
dh	ذ ذ ذ*	ـذ	ـذ	ذ	Dhāl	ذال ذ
r	ر ر ر*	ـر	ـر	ر	Rā'	راء ر
z	ز ز ز*	ـز	ـز	ز	Zāy	زاي ز
s	سسس	ـس	ـسـ	سـ	Sīn	سين س
sh	ششش	ـش	ـشـ	شـ	Shīn	شين ش
ṣ	صصص	ـص	ـصـ	صـ	Ṣād	صاد ص
ḍ	ضضض	ـض	ـضـ	ضـ	Ḍād	ضاد ض
ṭ	ططط	ـط	ـطـ	طـ	Ṭā'	طاء ط
ḍh	ظظظ	ـظ	ـظـ	ظـ	DHā'	ظاء ظ
ᶜ or ع	ععع	ـع	ـعـ	عـ	ᶜayn	عَيْن ع
gh	غغغ	ـغ	ـغـ	غـ	Ghayn	غَيْن غ

f	ففف	ـف	ـفـ	فـ	Fā'	فاء	ف
q	ققق	ـق	ـقـ	قـ	Qāf	قاف	ق
k	ككك	ـك	ـكـ	كـ	Kāf	كاف	ك
l	للل	ـل	ـلـ	لـ	Lām	لام	ل
m	ممم	ـم	ـمـ	مـ	Mīm	ميم	م
n	ننن	ـن	ـنـ	نـ	Nūn	نون	ن
h	ههه	ـه	ـهـ	هـ	Hā'	هاء	ه
ū / oo	و و و*	ـو	ـو	و	Wāw	واو	و
ī / y	ييي	ـي	ـيـ	يـ	Yā'	ياء	ي

* Non-connecting letter are the letters that, under no circumstances, may be joined to the letter which follows.

Arabic vowels and pronunciation symbols

Introduction

The Arabic language is enriched by a variety of pronunciation and vocalization symbols to help you to read the script easily with both accuracy and precision. In Arabic, these symbols are called *harakāt* (الحَرَكات), i.e. 'motions'. In Arabic, a letter is described as either resting (i.e. silent without vowels) or moving (i.e. vocalized).

It is always recommended that before you start learning the alphabet letters, i.e. consonants, you need to learn how to recognize the different vowels and pronunciation signs Arabs use. Once you master these signs, you will become proficient in reading and deciphering the Arabic script easily and accurately.

Arabic vowels are of two types:

- **short vowels** (الحَرَكات القَصيرة) are mainly diacritic markers (i.e. small orthographic signs) usually placed above or below consonantal letters. They are generally not indicated and omitted in most texts. As you advance further in your learning of Arabic, you will become accustomed to reading Arabic without the short vowels;
- **long vowels** (الحَرَكات الطَّويلة) are lengthened and are normally twice the length of a short vowel. They are alphabetical letters that are always written after the consonants.

There are also **supplementary vowels** (الحَرَكات الإضافيَّة), but these are less frequently used and are composed of a mixture of diactritics and supplementary letters.

The Arabic script can appear in two ways:

- **fully vocalized script** including full pronunciation markers and signs, is mostly used in religious texts (e.g. the Qur'an) (see example below), children's literature elementary schoolbooks and textbooks for beginner learners of Arabic. Another usage of vowels is to help with the pronunciation of foreign and unusual words.

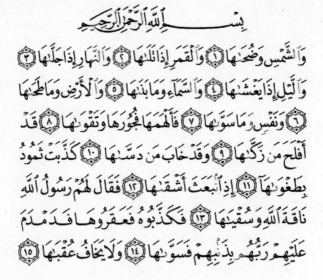

Extract from the Qur'an (The Sun 91, Chapter 15: 1–15)

- **non-vocalized script,** displaying only consonants without vowel signs, is usually used in normal handwriting and print style (e.g. newspapers and official documents – see example).

Excerpt from an Arabic newspaper

To help you with your reading, we have deliberately included vowels and pronunciation symbols in all the script in this book. However, as you progress further in Arabic, you will learn to predict the right pronunciation of words without the need for vowels, in the same way a native speaker does.

Note that a word in Arabic never begins with a vowel and a consonant is always pronounced before the vowel.

For teaching purposes and to demonstrate how you can pronounce these vowels correctly in combination with the letters, we will only be using the following consonantal letters:

1 Dāl (د) pronounced as /d/
2 Rā' (ر) pronounced as /r/
3 Sīn (س) pronounced as /s/
4 Mīm (م) pronounced as /m/.

The combination of the three root letters (d, r, s) i.e. د ر س bring about a wide collection of meaningful words that are connected to the topic of "studying and learning". This is a unique feature of the Arabic language and it will be covered later in Unit 15. Some combinations of d, r, s are meaningless and so will be utilized purely for reading practice purposes.

The letters د /d/ and ر /r/ are both non-connector letters (i.e. they connect only to preceding letters and not to the following ones). Their shape remains consistent whatever their position in a word, which makes their writing easier to learn at this stage of the book.

At the end of each unit, you will have many opportunities to practise writing the vowel signs and self-assess your learning.

Finally, to consolidate your reading of the vowels, the writing practice activities will be followed by reading tasks of vocalized letters as well as writing their phonetic equivalents in romanized Arabic.

Short vowels

Short vowels are small orthographic signs used predominantly in calligraphy and usually placed above or below consonantal letters. There are three short signs in Arabic: *Fatha* (فَتْحَة), *Damma* (ضَمَّة) and *Kasra* (كَسْرَة).

ـَ

Fatha (فَتْحَة) is a small diagonal stroke (ـَ) usually placed above a consonant. It is very common that the two dots of the Arabic letters (ت ق ي) are usually handwritten like a dash (ˉ) instead. Do not confuse this dash with the diagonal stroke of *Fatha* (ـَ).

Fatha

فَتْحَة

/a/

The vowel *Fatha* (فَتْحَة) is transliterated as /a/ and pronounced like:

1 /a/ as in m<u>a</u>t
2 /e/ as in b<u>u</u>t
3 /æ/ as in c<u>a</u>t

EXAMPLE

Pronounced as	Translation	Arabic
/da/ in <u>da</u>sh	-	دَ = ـَ + د ←
/darasa/	to study	دَرَسَ

ٝ

Damma (ضَمَّة) is a miniature shape of the Arabic letter wāw (و) usually placed above a consonant (ـُ).

Damma

ضَمَّة

/u/

The shape of Damma also can be described as a tiny comma (,) with a small circle at the top.

It is transliterated as /u/ and pronounced like:

1 /u/ in h<u>oo</u>d or
2 /o/ as in c<u>oo</u>k

Pronounced as	Translation	Arabic
/du/ in Dominique	-	دُ = ُ + د ←
/durisa/	was studied	دُرِسَ
/durasa/	-	دُرَسَ
/darusa/	-	دَرُسَ

Kasra (كَسْرَة) is a small diagonal stroke (ِ) similar to the *Fatha* (فَتْحَة) sign but placed below a consonant. It is transliterated as /i/ and pronounced like:

Kasra

كَسْرَة

1 /i/ in *hit* or
2 /e/ in *ship*.

/i/ EXAMPLES

Pronounced as	Translation	Arabic
/di/ as dish	-	دِ = ِ + د ←
/durisa/	was studied	دُرِسَ
/darisa/	-	دَرِسَ
/dirusa/	-	دِرُسَ

Writing practice
Practise tracing the following and copy.

Fatha (فَتْحَة)

_____ ﹷ ﹷ ﹷ ﹷ
_____ دَ دَ دَ دَ دَ

Damma (ضَمَّة)

_____ ﹹ ﹹ ﹹ ﹹ
_____ دُ دُ دُ دُ

Kasra (كَسْرَة)

_____ ﹻ ﹻ ﹻ ﹻ
_____ دِ دِ دِ دِ

Reading practice

To consolidate your reading and recognition of the **short vowels**, first practise reading the vocalized letters out loud and then write their phonetic equivalents in transliteration.

دِرَسَ دَرَسَ دِرُسَ دُرَسَ دَرِسَ دُرِسَ دَرِسَ دَرَسَ دِ دِ دِ دَ دَ دُ دَ دِ دُ دُ دُ دِ دَ دَ دِ دَ دَ دِ

Long vowels

The long vowels are the letters *Alif* (ا), *Wāw* (و) and *Yā'* (ي). These vowels are lengthened and are normally twice the length of a short vowel. As a phonetic guide, these vowels are transliterated in roman script as:

- /aa/ or /ā/ in f<u>a</u>ther
- /uu/ or /ū/ in m<u>oo</u>n
- /ii/ or /ī/ in s<u>ee</u>k.

ا	**Lengthening Alif** (أَلِف المَدَ). The first long vowel is *Alif* (ا) which is also the first letter of the Arabic alphabet. As well as a vowel, *Alif* also functions as a consonant. The consonantal function of *Alif* will be covered later (see Unit 1).
Lengthening Alif	This vowel lengthens the short vowel *Fatha* (فَتْحَة) /a/ (ﹷ) as the /a/ in f<u>a</u>ther.
أَلِف المَدَ *Alif Al-Madd* /aa/	The standalone letter *Alif* (ا), is written as a vertical stroke (ا), however in the medial and final form it is normally joined cursively to the right and appears as (ـا). *Alif* is considered as a non-connector letter and connects only to preceding letters to the right and not to the following ones on the left.
or /ā/	At this stage, you do not need to worry about joining letters. The letter *Dāl* د, which we are using as a sample consonant, is also a non-connector letter.

EXAMPLE

Pronounced as	Translation	Arabic
/dā/	-	دا = ا + د →
/dāris/	student	دارِس
/dārasa/	to study (together with s.o)	دارَسَ
/darasā/	they (dual) studied	دَرَسا
/dirāsah/	studying	دِراسَة
/madāris/	schools	مَدارِس

Lengthening Wāw (واو المَد). The second long vowel in alphabetical order is *Wāw* (و), which also functions as a consonant. The consonantal function of Wāw will be covered later.

Lengthening Wāw

This vowel lengthens the short vowel *Damma* (ضَمَّة) /u/ (ُ) as the /oo/ in m<u>oo</u>n.

واو المَد

Wāw Al-Madd

/uu/

or

/ū/

The standalone form of the letter *Wāw* (و) is written below the line as a wide angle with an oval loop (و), however in the medial and final form, it is normally joined cursively to the right and appears as ـو. *Wāw* is also considered as a non-connector letter and connects only to preceding letters to the right and not to the following ones to the left.

EXAMPLE

Pronounced as	Translation	Arabic
/dū/	-	دو = و + د →
/durūs/	lessons	دُروس
/madrūs/	studied	مَدُروس

ي

Lengthening Yā'

ياء المَد

(Yā Al-Madd)

/ii/

or

/ī/

Lengthening Yā' (ياء المَد). The third long vowel, which is the last letter of the alphabet table, is *Yā'* (ي).

This letter also functions as a consonant. The consonantal function of Yā' will be covered later.

This vowel lengthens the short vowel *Kasra* (كَسرَة) /i/ (ـِ) as the /ee/ in b<u>ee</u>.

The standalone form of the letter *Yā'* (ي), is written below the line as the letter "S" but with a curlier tail (ي).

Because *Yā'* (ي) is in, a fact, a connector letter (i.e. it connects both to the preceding and following letters):

1 The medial form appears as (ـيـ)
2 The final form keeps more or less the same original shape but joined to the right (ـي).

For the purpose of this section, you need only remember the standalone form of the letter *Yā'* (ي).

EXAMPLE

Pronounced as	Translation	Arabic
/dī/	-	دي = ي + د ←
/darsī/	my lesson	دَرْسِي (دَرْس + ي)
/madāris/	schools	مَدارِسِي (مَدارِس + ي)

Writing practice
Practise tracing the following and copy.

Lengthening Alif (أَلِف المَد)

_____ ‫ا ‫ ‫ا ‫ا ‫ا

_____ ‫ا د ‫ا د ‫ا د ‫ا د

Lengthening Wāw (واو المَد)

و ووو

دو دو دو دو

Lengthening Ya' (ياء المَد)

ي ي ي ي

دي دي دي دي

Reading practice

To consolidate your reading and recognition of the **long vowels**, first practise reading the vocalized letters out loud and then write their phonetic equivalents in transliteration.

دا دو دي   دو دا دو   دي دا دي   دا داِرس   دارَسَ   دَرَسا

دِراسَة   مَدارِس   دُروس   مَدُروس   دَرْسي   مَدارِسي

OTHER LONG VOWELS

The following vowel letters and symbols also lengthen the /a/ sound into /ā/ exactly like the vowel *Alif* (١).

Alif Maqṣūra

أَلِف مَقْصورة

/aa/

or

/ā/

Alif Maqsūra (أَلِف مَقْصورة) is written like the letter Yā' (ي) but without the two dots below. Hence, its other name (أَلِف بصورَة الياء *Alif biṣūrati al-yā'*), i.e. *Alif in the shape of Yā'*. Remember that *Alif Maqṣūra* is always placed at the end of a word.

It is transliterated and pronounced exactly like a lengthened *Alif* (/ā/).

EXAMPLE

Pronounced as	Translation	Arabic
/dā/	-	د + ى = دى
/sarā/	to set out	سَرى
/Musā/	Moses	موسى
/Isā/	Isāc	عيسى

Madda (مَدَّة) literally means lengthening and is written as a wavy sign (~).

In Modern Standard Arabic, *Madda* mostly appears above *Alif*, hence the other name **Alif Madda** (أَلِف مَدَّة).

Madda

مَدَّة

or

EXAMPLES

Pronounced as	Translation	Arabic
/dā/	-	د + آ = دآ
/āmīn/	amen	آمين
/al-'ān/	now	الآن
/Al-Qur'ān/	the Qur'an	القُرْآن

In Qur'anic script, it is used extensively above any consonant to lengthen its pronunciation (see example).

Alif Madda

أَلِف مَدَّة

/aal/

or

/āl/

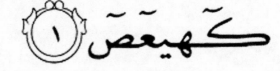

Kāf – Hā' – Yā' – ᶜayn – Sād

Extract from the Qur'an (Mary 19:1)

١

Dagger Alif (ٰ) (أَلِف مَخْفِيَّة), the last lengthening vowel, is an old pronunciation symbol that has survived up to today, although sometimes it is omitted hence its second name *hidden Alif* (أَلِف مَخْفِيَّة). It is also called *dagger Alif* (أَلِف خَنْجَرِيَّة) because of its typical shape.

―

Dagger Alif

أَلِف خَنْجَرِيَّة

(Alif Khanjariyya)

Hidden Alif

أَلِف مَخْفِيَّة

(Alif Makhfiyya)

/aa/ or /ā/

It is a miniature *Alif* (ٰ) usually written above consonants. It is usually used with a few frequent words in standard Arabic, however, it is commonly utilized in Qur'anic script as a substitute for the long vowel *Alif* (ا).

EXAMPLES

Pronounced as	Translation	Arabic
/dā/	–	دٰ = (ٰ) + د
/Allāh/	God	اللّٰه
/hādhā/	this (m)	هٰذا
/lākin/	but	لٰكن

Writing practice
Practise tracing the following and copy.

Alif Maqsura (أَلِف مَقْصورة)

ى   ى ى ى

دى   دى دى دى

Madda (مَدَّة)

ٓ   ٓ ٓ ٓ

دٓ   دٓ دٓ دٓ

Alif Madda (أَلِف مَدَّة)

آ   آ آ آ

دآ   دآ دآ دآ

Dagger Alif (أَلِف مَخْفِيَّة)

ٰ   ٰ ٰ ٰ

دٰ   دٰ دٰ دٰ

Supplementary vowels

DOUBLE VOWELLING: NUNATION (TANWEEN تَنْوِين)

In Arabic, we have a case of doubling the three short vowels (*Fatha* (فَتْحَة), *Danma* (ضمة) and Kasra (كَسْرَة)), which is called *Tanween* (تَنْوِين) or nunation in English.

Tanween (تَنْوِين) signs are always placed at the end of a word. There are three nunation signs:

1 *Fathatān* (ناتَحْتَف) i.e. double Fatha, pronounced as /an/
2 *Dammatān* (ضَـمَّتان) i.e. double Damma, pronounced as /un/
3 *Kasratān* (كَسْرَتان) i.e. double Kasra, pronounced as /in/.

The Arabic suffix (-ān) in three names *Fathatān*, *Dammatān* and *Kasratān* stands for the dual case.

Normally, whenever the double vowel signs are used, they indicate indefiniteness and singularity, i.e. that a word takes the indefinite article (e.g. a car, a book, etc.) and/or is singular.

Grammatically speaking, the three types of nunation also signify three case endings: accusative /an/, nominative /un/ and indicative /in/.

	Fathatān (ناتَحْتَف), (i.e. double *Fatha*), is written as a double diagonal stroke (ـً) above the consonant.
Double Fatha	It is mostly written in combination with *Alif* (l) as لَ or (ةً) *Ta' Marbūṭa*. It is transliterated and pronounced as /an/ and it is always placed at the end of a word.

فَتْحَتان

Fathatān

/an/

EXAMPLE

Pronounced as	Translation	Arabic
/dan/	–	آد = آ + د →
/darsan/	lesson	دَرْساً
/madrasatan/	school	مَدْرَسَةً

Grammatically speaking, the nunation (فَتْحَتان) /an/ represents a case ending called the accusative.

ٌو

—

or

ٌى

—

*Double
Damma*

/un/

Dammatān (ضَمَّتان), (i.e. double *Damma*), is written
as a double *Damma* sign (ٌ) or a special *sign* (ٌ)
always above the consonant.

It is transliterated and pronounced as /un/ and it is
always placed at the end of a word.

EXAMPLE

Pronounced as	Translation	Arabic
/dun/	-	دٌ = (ٌ) + د → ←
/darsun/	lesson	دَرْسٌ
/madrasatun/	school	مَدْرَسَةٌ

Grammatically speaking, the nunation (ضَمَّتان) /un/
represents a case ending known as the nominative.

≠

—

*Double
Kasra*

كَسْرَتان

Kasratān

/in/

Kasratān (كَسْرَتان), (i.e. double *kasra*), is written as a
double diagonal stroke (ٍ) below the consonant.

It is transliterated and pronounced as /in/ and it is
always placed at the end of a word.

EXAMPLE

Pronounced as	Translation	Arabic
/din/	-	دٍ = (ٍ) + د → ←
/darsin/	Lesson	دَرْسٍ
/madrasatin/	School	مَدْرَسَةٍ

Grammatically speaking, the nunation (كَسْرَتان) /in/
represents a case ending called the indicative.

Writing practice

Practise tracing the following and copy.

Fathatān (فَتْحَتان)

دَاً دَاً دَاً دَاً

Dammatān (ضَـمَّتان)

دٌ دٌ دٌ دٌ

Kasratān (كَسْرَتان)

دٍ دٍ دٍ دٍ

Reading practice

To consolidate your reading and recognition of **Tanween** signs, first practise reading the vocalized letters out loud and then write their phonetic equivalents in transliteration.

دَاً دِ دٌ دَاً دُ دِ دَاً دِ دٌ دَرْساً دَرْسٌ دَرْسٍ مَدْرَسَةً مَدْرَسَةٌ مَدْرَسَةٍ

FURTHER SUPPLEMENTARY VOWELS

ه

▬

Absence vowel

Sukūn

Sukūn (سُكون) is written as a small circle (ـْ) above consonants. In Arabic, the *Sukūn* literally means silence or quiescence, indicating an absence of a vowel and a silence of the consonant.

A consonant with *Sukūn* is called a vowelless letter. This means that a consonant is pronounced alone without any other sound.

سُكون

/no transliteration/

The *Sukūn* is normally transliterated with the letter carrying the Sukūn (سُكون) sign and pronounced like the vowelless letter "n" in Lo<u>n</u>don, Ma<u>n</u>chester and Engla<u>nd</u>.

EXAMPLE

Pronounced as	Translation	Arabic
/d/ as in ma<u>d</u>	-	دْ = (ـْ) د +
/darsun/	lesson	دَرْسٌ
/madrasatun/	school	مَدْرَسَةٌ

In Qur'an script, the *Sukūn* is written as as semi-closed circle:

( )

Writing practice
Practise tracing the following and copy.

Reading practice
To consolidate your reading and recognition of the **Sukūn** sign, first practise reading the vocalized letters out loud and then write their phonetic equivalents in transliteration.

مَدْرَسَةٌ دَرْسِي دَرْسٌ دْ

ش

―――――

Shadda

شَدَّة

or

Tashdīd

تَشْدِيد

/doubled consonant/

Shadda (شَدَّة) **or Tashdīd** (تَشْدِيد) is written as a miniature w sign above consonants (ـّ). In Arabic, *Shadda* literally means intensifying and reinforcement. It indicates a replacement of double consonants, which are never written in Arabic.

It is transliterated as a double consonant e.g. /dd/ and pronounced with a heavy stress and strong emphasis on the consonant being doubled.

For instance, notice how you pronounce "c" in a<u>cc</u>ommodation and "d" in mo<u>d</u>ernity.

───

Shadda (ـّ) can occur together with other vowel signs:

1 with the three short vowels /a/, /u/ and /i/, as follows: (ـُّ ـَّ ـِّ)
2 with the three double vowels of nunation (/an/, /un/, /in/) as follows (ـٌّ ـًّ ـٍّ)
3 with the Dagger *Alif* as in (الله *Allāh*) i.e. God.

Note that the *Shadda* is usually omitted in non-vocalized script.

All sun letters must have a *Shadda* when preceded by the definite article (الـ). (See Unit 1 for further details.)

───

When the *Shadda* is combined with *Kasra* /i/, the latter is placed below either the *Shadda* (ـِّ) or the consonant. (ـِّ).

EXAMPLES

Read the following letter/vowel combinations, starting from right to left.

Pronounced as	Arabic
/dda/	دَّ ←
/ddu/	دُّ
/ddi/	دِّ
/ddā/	دَّا
/ddū/	دُّو
/ddī/	دِّي
/ddan/	دًّا
/ddun/	دٌّ
/ddin/	دٍّ

Writing practice

Practise tracing the following and copy.

ـَ ـَ ـَ ـَ

دَ دَ دَ دَ

دُ دُ دُ دُ

دِ دِ دِ دِ

دٌ دٌ دٌ دٌ

دَاً دَاً دَاً دَاً

دٍ دٍ دٍ دٍ

Reading practice

To consolidate your reading and recognition of the **Shadda** vowel, first practise reading the vocalized letters out loud and then write their phonetic equivalents in transliteration.

دَ دُ دِ دُ دَ دَا دَّي دَاً دَّ دَّ دَّ دَرَّسَ مُدَرِّس مُدَرِّسَةٌ

DIPHTHONGS

Diphthongs are vowel sounds represented by the combination of a short vowel /a/ (*Fatha*) and either of the two consonants و or ي.

The first diphthong is a combination of the vowel (/a/ *fatha*) and the consonant *Wāw* (و) carrying a Sukūn (سكون) vowel (ـْ) above it.

It is transliterated as /aw/ and pronounced as /aw/ in *how* and *mouse*

diphthong 1

/aw/

EXAMPLES

Pronounced as	Translation	Arabic
/daw/	-	دَوْ = دَ + ـوْ ← د
/dawr/	role	دَوْر
/daws/	-	دَوْس
/dawd/	-	دَوْد
/yawm/	day	يَوْم
/qawl/	speech	قَوْل

The second diphthong is a combination of the vowel (/a/ *Fatha*) and the consonant *Yā'* (ي) carrying a *Sukūn* (سكون) vowel (ﹱ) above it.

Diphthong 2

It is transliterated and pronounced as /ay/ in *my* and *mile*.

/ail/ or /ay/

EXAMPLES

Pronounced as	Translation	Arabic
/day/	-	د + ﹷيْ = دَيْ ←
/days/	-	دَيْس
/dayru/	-	دَيْر
bayt	house	بَيْت
shaykh	old man	شَيْخ
jayb	pocket	جَيْب

Writing practice
Practise tracing the following and copy.

ﹷوْ ﹷوْ ﹷوْ ﹷوْ

دَوْ دَوْ دَوْ دَوْ

ﹷيْ ﹷيْ ﹷيْ ﹷيْ

دَيْ دَيْ دَيْ دَيْ

Reading practice
To consolidate your reading and recognition of the **diphthongs**, first practise reading the vocalized letters out loud and then write their phonetic equivalents in transliteration.

دَيْرٌ دَيْسٌ دَوْرٌ دَيْ دَوْ

← دَ دا دَّ دُ دي دَيْ دَ دْ دُ دآ دَوْ

دُّ دَ دْ دِ دَّ دآ دى دِ دَّ دْ دُ دآ دو

دَوْ دَ دَ دا داً دِ دُّدُ دَيْ دَ داً دْ دِ دَّ دآ

In a nutshell

The tables that follow present summaries of the names, shapes, pronunciation and usage of all the vowels and pronunciation symbols covered so far.

Name of vowel		Shape	Pronunciation and transliteration	Example and pronunciation	
English	Arabic				
Short vowels					
Fatha	فَتْحَة	ـَ	/a/ in c<u>a</u>t	دَ	/da/
Damma	ضَمَّة	ـُ	/u/ in f<u>u</u>ll	دُ	/du/
Kasra	كَسْرَة	ـِ	/i/ in s<u>i</u>t	دِ	/di/
Long vowels					
Long Alif	ألِف المَدّ Alif Al-Madd	ا	/ā/ in f<u>a</u>ther	دا	/dā/
Long *Yāʾ*	ياء ألِف *Yāʾ* Al-Madd	ي	/ī/ in s<u>ee</u>n	دي	/dī/
Long *Wāw*	واو المَدّ *Wāw* Al-Madd	و	/ū/ in m<u>oo</u>n	دو	/dū/
Shortened Alif	ألِف مَقْصورة Alif Maqsura	ى	/ā/ in f<u>a</u>ther	دى	/bā/
Dagger/ hidden Alif	ألِف خَنْجَرِيَّة/ مَخْفِيَّة Alif Khanjariyya/ Makhfiyya	ـٰ	/ā/ in f<u>a</u>ther	دٰ	/dā/
Alif Madda or Madda	ألِف مَدَّة مَدَّة	آ ـٓ	/ā/ in f<u>a</u>ther	دٓ	/dā/

Supplementary vowels

Double Fatha	فَتْحَتان Fathatān	ـً	/an/	دأ	/dan/
Double Damma	ضَمَّتان Dammatān	ـٌ or ـٌ	/un/	دٌ	/dun/
Double Kasra	كَسْرَتان Kasratān	ـٍ	/in/	دٍ	/din/
Consonant doubling	شَدَّة/ تَشْديد Shadda/ Tashdīd	ـّ	(double consonant) as the emphasized /c/ in a<u>cc</u>ommodation	دّ	/dd/
Vowellessness	سُكون Sukūn	ـْ	/absence of vowel/ (no transliteration)	دْ	/d/
Diphthong 1 (aw)	فَتْحَة + واو Fatha + Wāw	ـَوْ	/aw/ in h<u>ow</u>	دَوْ	/daw/
Diphthong 2 (ay)	فَتْحَة + ياء Fatha + Yā'	ـَيْ	/ay/ in m<u>i</u>ne	دَيْ	/day/

•••

L

Unit 1

Letter group no. 1

Alif أَلِف /'/

Lām لام /l/

Hamza الهَمْزَة /'/

ا
Isolated

ل
Isolated

ء
Isolated

ل	ا	ـل	ـلـ	ل	ئ	ؤ	أ إ آ
Final/Medial	Initial	Final	Medial	Initial	Final	Medial	Initial

In this unit you will learn
- *how to read and write the letters ل and ا*
- *combination of ا and ل*
- *new words using these two letters*

The first letter group is very easy and straightforward to learn. The group consists of two important consonantal letters you should learn before tackling any other letters. The two letters are Alif أَلِف (ا) and Lām لام (ل), which both share the shape of a vertical downward stroke. The Hamza sign is not usually considered an alphabetical letter and will be explained along with the letter Alif.

Letter group no. 1 in a nutshell

Pronunciation	Joined up	Final	Medial	Initial	Isolated	Name of the Arabic letter
/′/ in and	لا	ـل	ـلـ	ا	ا	أَلِف Alif
/l/ in lamb	لل	ـل	ـلـ	ل	ل	لام Lām

HOW TO WRITE IT

In the following activity, you will learn how to write ا and ل in different positions. Then you will practise writing all these positions connected in one imaginary word.

Skeleton shape

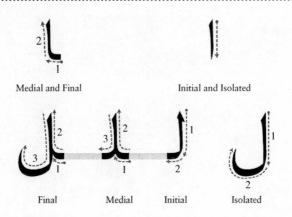

Medial and Final   Initial and Isolated

Final   Medial   Initial   Isolated

Following the diagram of the skeleton shape, practise tracing the following and copy on the line, working from right to left.

Letter Alif

←

_____ ١١١   ا

_____ للل   ل

Letter Lām

←	ل	
ل	ل ل ل	_____
ل	ل ل ل	_____
ل	ل ل ل	_____
ل	ل ل ل ل	_____
لل	لل لل لل	_____

IN DIFFERENT CALLIGRAPHIC STYLES

This is how Lām (ل) is written in different script and calligraphy styles.

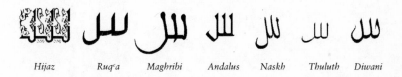

Hijaz	Ruqʿa	Maghribi	Andalus	Naskh	Thuluth	Diwani

The letter Alif حَرْفُ الأَلِف

Alif أَلِف	Hamza الهَمْزَة
/ʾ/	/ʾ/
ا	ﻉ
Isolated	Isolated

Final and Medial	Initial		Final	Medial	Initial
ﺎ	ﺃ		أ إ آ	ﺆ	ﺋ ﺊ

The letter Alif (along with two other letters) can function as either consonant or vowel. Alif as a vowel was covered earlier.

Alif ألف (١) is the first letter of the Arabic alphabet and is probably the most commonly used in Arabic writing. It is written as a vertical stroke similar to the roman "l". It is one of the six non-connector letters and connects only to the preceding letters to the right and not to the following ones to the left.

It serves two purposes:

1 it can appear as a vowel pronounced as /aa/ in "father";
2 or a consonant, which usually carries the non-alphabetical sign, Hamza (ء).

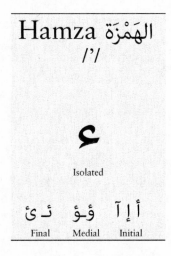

The Hamza has a reputation of having complicated rules of writing and reading that are beyond the scope of this book. However, to keep the Hamza as simple as possible, here are a few essentials to remember:

1 Hamza is considered as an additional sign and not as part of the Arabic alphabet.

2 Hamza can appear either alone resting on the writing line or carried by the letters Alif (ا), Wāw (و) or Yā' (ي). These letters are usually referred to as "Hamza seats".

3 The Hamza cannot be joined to any letter, regardless of its position. But, when carried by any of the three "seats", the latter take the appropriate form depending on its position.

4 Although the Hamza is mostly ignored in everyday writing, in both handwriting and print, we will use it throughout the book whenever it occurs.

5 Bear in mind that, in Arabic, there is no word that begins with a vowel. So, when you see a word beginning with Alif (with or without the Hamza), you should always assume that there is a Hamza above vowel Alif, even if it's not written.

6 At the beginning of any word, Hamza is always written either above (أ) or below Alif (إ).

7 Further examples of Hamza in real context will be shown later when it is in combination with other letters, and more explanations will be given as required.

Hamza variations in a nutshell

Final	Medial	Initial	Isolated	Hamza in different positions
ـأ	ـأـ	أ	أ	Above Alif
-	-	إ	إ	Below Alif
ـؤ	ـؤـ	-	ؤ	Above Wāw
ـئ	ـئـ	-	ئ	Above Yā'
ء	-	-	ء	Resting on the line (level with the other letters)

HOW TO WRITE IT

Practise tracing the following and copy on the line, working from right to left.

←

————————————————————————— ء ء ء   ء

————————————————————————— أ أ أ   أ

————————————————————————— إ إ إ   إ

HOW TO READ IT

The sound of Hamza is not an unfamiliar sound to the European ear. To give you a hint of how Hamza is pronounced by Arabs, try pronouncing the following words in a Cockney accent! The letters underlined are where the Hamza sound occurs:

Ma<u>t</u>e   Bu<u>tt</u>er   That's <u>it</u>   I<u>n</u>ternet   Sco<u>tt</u>ish   <u>A</u>mazing   A<u>n</u>xious   <u>A</u>we

Here is another example. Pronounce the following sentence with the same accent:

Put a little bit of butter on it mate!
/ Pu' a li'ile bi' o bu'er on i' ma'e! /

Did you notice a catch in the throat when you pronounced those words? That's what linguists call a "glottal stop" where you have to pause for a short while to produce the sound of Hamza.

To sum up, Hamza is pronounced exactly as a short vowel i.e. /a/, /u/ or /i/ and it is mostly transliterated with an apostrophe (') followed by a short or long vowel. In Arabic, it is written with special small sign: ء.

Alif Madda

If you remember, in the **Vowels and pronunciation symbols** section earlier, we covered the **Madda sign** (~), which lengthens the pronunciation of consonants.

However, in Modern Standard Arabic (MSA), Madda mostly appears above the letter Alif, hence the name Alif Madda (أَلِف مَدَّة).

Alif Madda is simply a lengthened أ i.e.:

$$آ = ١ + أ$$

With long vowels

Read the following letter/vowel combinations, working from right to left.

Supplementary vowels		Double vowels		Long vowels		Short vowels	
/aa/	أ	/an/	اً	/ā/ آ=١+أ		/a/	أ
vowelless /'/	أْ	/un/	اٌ	/ū/ أو		/u/	أُ
/ā/	أى	/in/	اٍ	/ī/ إي		/i/	إ

The letter Lām حَرْفُ اللّام

لام Lām
/l/

ل

Isolated

ـل   ـلـ   لـ

Final   Medial   Initial

The second letter in this group is Lām لام (ل). It is the twenty-third letter of the alphabet. Lām (ل) is a connector letter that can be joined up from both its sides with four different shapes reflecting each position. It shares the shape of a vertical downstroke similar to the roman letter "l" which also resembles the letter Alif (ا). However, Lām (ل) is connected cursively from both sides.

Lām (ل) can be combined with Alif (ا) to form two distinct well-known Arabic letter combinations: لا and لا.

HOW TO READ IT

ل is transliterated and pronounced as /l/ as in the word *lamb*. Notice how ل is sounded in combination with the different vowels and pronunciation symbols in the following table.

Read the following letter/vowel combinations, working from right to left.

Supplementary vowels		Double vowels		Long vowels		Short vowels	
/ll/	لّ	/lan/	لاً	/lā/	لا	/la/	لَ
vowelless /l/	لْ	/lun/	لٌ	/lū/	لو	/lu/	لُ
/lā/	لى	/lin/	لٍ	/lī/	لي	/li/	لِ

COMBINATION OF LĀM ل AND ALIF ا

Combination 1: negative pronoun in Arabic (لا)

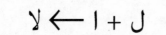

$$ لا \longleftarrow ا + ل $$

The combination of ا + ل leads to a special distinctive shape of لا, which is not considered part of the alphabet. There are two types of لا:

1. If ل is connected to the <u>vowel Alif</u> ا, if isolated, the combination لا conveys the meaning of "no" and is considered one of the negation nouns in Arabic. لا in this case is transliterated and pronounced as /lā/.

2 If ل is connected to the <u>consonant Alif</u> أ or إ, this is explained further in this unit under "Sun and moon letters".

Remember that because Alif is a non-connector letter, لا cannot connect in writing to any following letter, as in these examples:

الإِثْنَين	الأَب	لا إِلـه	ثَلاثة	حَلال	الثُّلاثاء	أوْلاد
Monday	Father	There is no God	Three	Permitted	Tuesday	Children
al-'ithnayn	al-'ab	lā 'ilāha	thalāthah	halāl	a(l)th-thulāthā'	'awlād

Following the diagram of the skeleton shape, practise tracing the following and copy on the line, working from right to left.

Skeleton shape

Medial and Final | Isolated

←

لا لا لا   لا

Print form

لا لا لا   لا

Handwritten form

IN DIFFERENT CALLIGRAPHIC STYLES

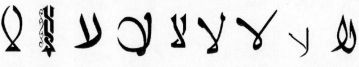

Qairwan Hijaz Ruqʿa Maghribi Andalus Naskh 1 Naskh 2 Thuluth Diwani

Combination 2: the definite article in Arabic (ال)

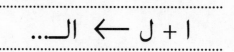

Most of the time, when Alif ا (as a consonant) precedes Lām ل, it is most likely to be the definite article similar to "the" in English.

It is commonly transliterated as "al-" (the dash indicating that "al" is not part of the word) and pronounced in two different ways depending on the type of the first consonantal letter: sun or moon letter.

Before we move on to the next set of consonants, you must be aware that Arabic consonants are divided into two categories (including exactly 14 letters in each):

1 sun letters   الحُروف الشَّمْسِيَّة
2 moon letters   الحُروف القَمَرِيَّةَ.

SUN LETTERS   الحُروف الشَّمْسِيَّة

ت ث د ذ ر ز س ش ص ض ط ظ ل ن

When ال is attached to any word that begins with a sun letter, the pronunciation of ال is affected, i.e. the ل of ال becomes silent and assimilated into the word. As a result, the first consonant after ال becomes doubled, i.e. carrying a Shaddah sign (ــّـ).

Pronunciation

a(l)- + double consonant		sun letter
(l) of ال is silent and assimilated into the word	←	حَرْف شَمْسِيّ + الــ

Examples

السودان	سودان←	الثُّلاثاء	ثُلاثاء←	الشَّمْس	شَمْس←
a(l)s-sūdān	*sūdān*	*a(l)th-thulathā'*	*thulathā'*	*a(l)sh-shams*	*shams*
Sudan	Sudan	Tuesday	Tuesday	The sun	Sun

MOON LETTERS الحُروف القَمَرِيَّة

أ ب ج ح خ ع غ ف ق ك م و ي ه

When ال is attached to any word that begins with a moon letter, ل of ال is pronounced normally as (al-) followed by the word.

Regarding the combination لا, if ل is connected to the consonant Alif ا or إ, it is pronounced as /al- / followed by أ /a/, إ /i/ or أُ /u/ as in Monday الإِثْنَين /al-ithnayn/.

More examples will follow later using other Arabic letters.

Pronunciation

al- + consonant letter (ل is pronounced)	←	moon letter حَرْف قَمَرِيّ	الـ +

Examples

العَرَبِيَّة	عَرَبِيَّة←	الأَب	أَب←	القَمَر	قَمَر←
al-ʿarabiyyah	*ʿarabiyyah*	*al-'ab*	*'ab*	*al-qamar*	*qamar*
The Arabic (language)	Arabic (language)	The father	Father	The moon	Moon

Insight

You already speak Arabic!

If you are an English speaker, you have certainly come across words like alcohol, algebra, alchemy, algorithm and albatross.

Do you notice that they all start with (al-)?

Would you be surprised to know that they all originate from Arabic?

These words – among thousands – are called Arabic loanwords, which have been borrowed by the English language through other European languages. Here are some examples.

Arabic loanwords	Pronunciation	Arabic equivalent	Meaning
Examples beginning with **moon letters**			
alcohol	al-kuhl	الكُحْل	powder used as an eyeliner
algebra	al-jabr	الجَبر	restoring missing parts
alchemy	al-kīmyā'	الكيمْياء	originally from medieval Latin
algorithm	al-khawārizmī	الخَوارِزمي	surname of a Muslim mathematician
albatross	al-ghaṯṯās	الغَطّاس	diver
admiral	amīr al-bihār	أميرُالبِحار	commander of the seas
Examples beginning with **sun letters**			
adobe	a(l)ṯ-ṯūb	الطّوب	brick
arsenal	dār a(l)s-sināʿah	دار الصِّناعَة	house of manufacturing

IN DIFFERENT CALLIGRAPHIC STYLES

الا الا أُل الّ الـ الا ال الـ ال ال

Qairwan   Hijaz   Ruqʿa   Maghribi   Andalus   Naskh 1   Naskh 2   Thuluth   Diwani

OTHER COMBINATIONS OF ا AND ل

interrogative noun to ask yes or no questions e.g. Are you...?	ʾa	_____ أ	أ	أ
to (preposition)	ʾilā	إل ى إلى _____	إلى	إلى
except, other than	ʾillā	إلاَّ إل أ _____	إلاَّ	إلاَّ
don't you...?	ʾalā	ألا إل أ _____	ألا	ألا
family	ʾāl	آل آ ل _____	آل	آل

ARABIC QUOTE حِكْمَة عَرَبِيَّة

خَيْرُ الكَلامِ ما قَلَّ وَدَلَّ وَلَمْ يَطُلْ فَيُمِلّ

khayru al-kalām mā qalla wa dalla wa qm yutil fayumill
The best speech is that which is short and meaningful

Arabic proverb

Circle the letters ل and the combinations of Alif and Lām
wherever you see them in the quote.

SUMMARY TABLE

The following table is a summary of what you need to know about the letters ل ا and their combinations.

Pronun- ciation	Joined up	Final	Medial	Initial	Isolated		Name
'	ااا	ـا	ـا	ا	ا	أَلِف	Alif
l	الل	ـل	ـلـ	لـ	ل	لام	Lām

Alif-Lām combinations

					Name
Negation noun	لا	ل + ا	لام-أَلِف	Lām-Alif
Definite article	الـ ...	ا + ل	أَلِف-لام	Alif-Lām

Test yourself

Exercise 1
Read out loud and combine the letters to form words.

ل و	ل ي	لا	ل ا
إ ل ى	أ ل ا	ل ى	
إ ل ى	أل أ او	إ ي	

Exercise 2
Read out loud and write the unjoined forms of the letters that make up the following words.

أَلا   إِلَّا   إِلى

Exercise 3
Transliterate the words in Exercises 1 and 2 into roman script.

Exercise 4

Can you recognize the combination لا in the calligraphic writings above?

Unit **2**

الوِحْدَة الثّانِيَة

....

Letter group no. 2

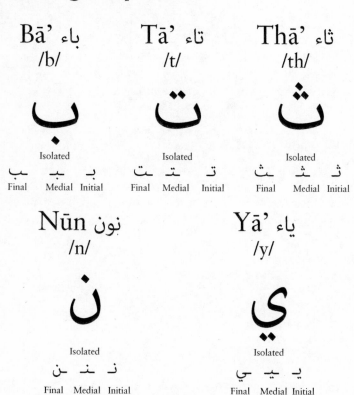

Bāʾ باء
/b/

ب

Isolated

ـب ـبـ بـ
Final Medial Initial

Tāʾ تاء
/t/

ت

Isolated

ـت ـتـ تـ
Final Medial Initial

Thāʾ ثاء
/th/

ث

Isolated

ـث ـثـ ثـ
Final Medial Initial

Nūn نون
/n/

ن

Isolated

ـن ـنـ نـ
Final Medial Initial

Yāʾ ياء
/y/

ي

Isolated

ـي ـيـ يـ
Final Medial Initial

In this unit you will learn

- *how to write and join the letters* ب ت ث ن ي
- *how to read and recognize these letters in a real context in a variety of script styles*
- *new and commonly used vocabulary using these letters*

16

This second letter group consists of the highest number of letters that share exactly the same skeleton shape and writing pattern, mainly in the isolated, initial and medial positions. The only difference between these letters is the number and location of dots they carry. Bear in mind that these dots are an integral feature of the letter and cannot be omitted, unlike the diactric vowels.

This group can be divided into two sub-groups:

Sub-group 1
The letters ب ت ث all share the same skeleton shape in all four positions. The shape is similar to that of a wide kayak. These letters are distinguished only by the number of dots, which are either above or below the letter (see table).

Joined up	Final	Medial	Initial	Isolated	Name of the Arabic letter	
ببب	ـب	ـبـ	بـ	ب	باء	Bā'
تتت	ـت	ـتـ	تـ	ت	تاء	Tā'
ثثث	ـث	ـثـ	ثـ	ث	ثاء	Thā'

Sub-group 2
The letters ن ي both share the skeleton shape of the main group, but only in the initial and medial positions. Unlike the letters ب ت ث, they have a unique script form in the isolated and final position (see table).

Joined up	Final	Medial	Initial	Isolated	Name of the Arabic letter	
يـيـي	ـي	ـيـ	يـ	ي	ياء	Yā'
نـنـن	ـن	ـنـ	نـ	ن	نون	Nūn

To illustrate the similarities between the five members of this letter group, compare the script in the different positions in these two tables.

The shaded sections highlight where the letters share the majority of their shape similarities.

HOW TO WRITE IT

In the following activity, you will learn how to write the skeleton shape of the letters ب ت ث, followed by ن ي in the four different positions.

Then you will practise writing the letters in all these positions connected in one imaginary word.

Start with the main shape, and then add the dots above the hook of the letter. Notice carefully where the dot is positioned: under the hook in the initial and medial positions and under the full shape in the isolated and final positions.

Following the diagram of the skeleton shape, practise tracing the following and copy on the line, working from right to left.

Skeleton shape

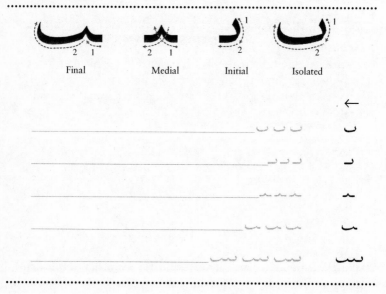

Final	Medial	Initial	Isolated

Now repeat the same writing exercise for the letters ث ت ب.

Notice where the dot(s) is positioned in each letter.

As a rule of thumb, the following will help you to remember the names and number of dots carried by each letter:

1 Bā' is similar to a bare boat (Bare Bā'!)
2 Tā' has two dots (Two Tā'!)
3 Thā' has three dots (Three Thā'!).

Sub-group 2

LETTER NŪN (ن)

The two letters Nūn (ن) and Bā' (ب) might look very similar initially. Make sure you remember where the dot of each letter positioned: above the letter in Nūn (ن) and below it in Bā' (ب).

Practise tracing the following and copy.

Skeleton shape

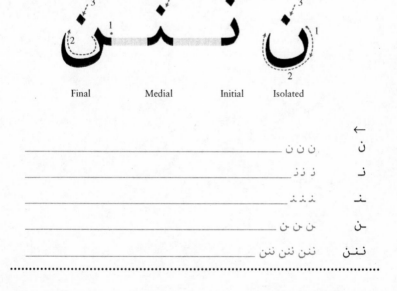

Final	Medial	Initial	Isolated

LETTER YĀ' (ي)

The standalone form of the letter Yā' (ي) is written below the line as the letter "S" but with a curlier tail (ي).

Practise tracing the following and copy.

Skeleton shape

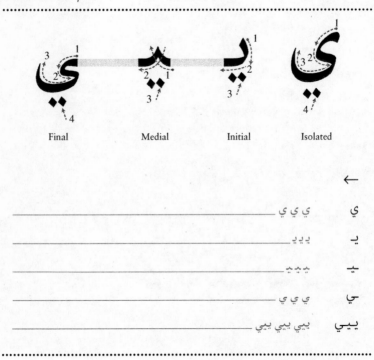

| Final | Medial | Initial | Isolated |

←

ي ي ي ي

ـيـ ـيـ ـيـ ـيـ

يـ يـ يـ يـ

ـي ـي ـي ـي

يـي يـي يـي يـي

The letter Bā' حَرْفُ الباء

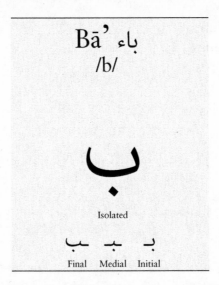

Bā' باء
/b/

ب

Isolated

ب   بـ   ـب
Final   Medial   Initial

The first letter of this group is Bā' باء ب, which is the second letter in the Arabic alphabet. It is a connector letter with four shapes, and it shares exactly the same shape and writing pattern of the skeleton shape with the difference of a dot below the letter (ب بـ ـبـ ـب).

Pronunciation	Joined up	Final	Medial	Initial	Isolated	Name
/b/ in boat	بیب	ـب	ـبـ	بـ	ب	Bā' باء

HOW TO READ IT

The letter Bā' is transliterated and pronounced as /b/ in the word _boat_. Notice how ب is sounded in combination with the different vowels and pronunciation symbols in the following table.

Read the following letter/vowel combinations.

Supplementary vowels		Double vowels		Long vowels		Short vowels	
/bb/	بّ	/ban/	باً	/bā/	با	/ba/	بَ
vowelless /b/	بْ	/bun/	بٌ	/bū/	بو	/bu/	بُ
/bā/	بى	/bin/	بٍ	/bī/	بي	/bi/	بِ

IN DIFFERENT CALLIGRAPHIC STYLES

This is how ب is written in different script and calligraphy styles. The letters ت ث will look exactly the same, with the exception of two dots above ت and three above ث.

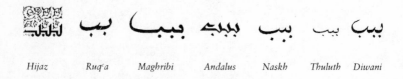

| Hijaz | Ruqʿa | Maghribi | Andalus | Naskh | Thuluth | Diwani |

READ AND WRITE IT IN REAL CONTEXTS

Look at how ب is combined with other letters from the previous letter groups.

Find out what letters these words are composed of, then join the combinations of letters as shown.

Start with the main shape, then add the dots followed by the vowels.

Translation	Pronunciation	Handwriting practice	Combinations	Print form
		←		

Reading direction
Practice tracing the following and copy.

With long vowels

Translation	Pronunciation	Handwriting practice	Combinations	Print form
-	bā	با	ب ا	با
-	bū	بو	ب و	بو
-	bī	بي	ب ي	بي

Translation	Pronunciation	Handwriting practice	Combinations	Print form
father (formal)	'ab	أب	أ ب	أب
my father	'abī	أبي	أ ب ي	أبي
Dad (informal)	bābā	بابا	ب ا ب ا	بابا
without	bilā	بلا	بِ ل ا	بِلا
door	bāb	باب	ب ا ب	باب
my door	bābī	بابي	ب ا ب ي	بابي
nightingale	bulbul	بُلْبُل	بُ لْ بُ ل	بُلْبُل
August	āb	آب	آ ب	آب

QUICK VOCAB

The letter Tāʼ حَرْفُ التَـاء

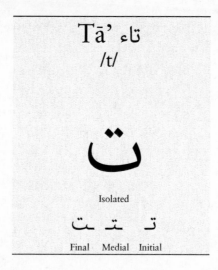

Tāʼ تاء
/t/

ت

Isolated

ت ـتـ ـت

Final   Medial   Initial

The second letter in this group is Tāʼ تاء ت, which is the third letter in the Arabic alphabet. It is the only letter with two dots above its skeleton shape (ت ـتـ ـت), while the last letter of this group (ي) has the dots below. Tāʼ (ت) is a connector letter that can be joined up from both its sides with four different shapes reflecting each position.

Pronunciation	Joined up	Final	Medial	Initial	Isolated	Name
/t/ in tea	تتت	ـت	ـتـ	تـ	ت	تاء Tāʼ

HOW TO READ IT

The letter Tāʼ (ت) is transliterated and pronounced as /t/ as in the word *tea*. Notice how ت is sounded in combination with the different vowels and pronunciation symbols in the following table.

Read the following letter/vowel combinations.

Supplementary vowels		Double vowels		Long vowels		Short vowels	
/tt/	تّ	/tan/	تاً	/tā/	تا	/ta/	تَ
vowelless /t/	ثْ	/tun/	تٌ	/tū/	تو	/tu/	تُ
/tā/	تى	/tin/	تٍ	/tī/	تي	/ti/	تِ

READ AND WRITE IT IN REAL CONTEXTS

Look at how ت is combined with other letters from the previous letter group. Find out what letters these words are composed of and then join the combinations of letters as shown.

Translation	Pronunciation	Handwriting practice	Combinations	Print form

←
Reading direction
Practise tracing the following and copy.

With long vowels

-	tā	_____ تا	ت ا	تا
-	tū	_____ تو	ت ي	تو
-	tī	_____ تي	ت و	تي

to repent	tāba	_____	تابَ	ت ا بَ	تابَ
she repented	tābat	_____	تابَتْ	ت ا بَ تْ	تابَتْ
repent!	tub	_____	تُبْ	تُ بْ	تُبْ
hill	tall	_____	تَلَ	تَ لَّ	تَلَّ
hills	tilāl	_____	تِلال	تِ ل ا ل	تِلال
mulberry	tūt	_____	توت	ت و ت	توت
to be	bāta	_____	باتَ	ب ا تَ	باتَ
she was	bātat	_____	باتَتْ	ب ا تَ تْ	باتَتْ

The letter Thā' حَرْفُ الثَّاء

The third letter in this group is Thā' ثاء (ث), which is the fourth letter in the alphabet. In Arabic, there are only two letters that carry three dots above: Thā' (ث) and Shīn (ش). Thā' (ث) is a connector letter that can be joined up from both its sides, with four different shapes reflecting these positions (ث ثـ ـثـ ـث).

Pronunciation	Joined up	Final	Medial	Initial	Isolated	Name
/th/ in three	ثث	ـث	ـثـ	ثـ	ث	ثاء Thā'

HOW TO READ IT

Thā' ثاء (ث) is transliterated and pronounced as /th/ in *thanks*, *Matthew* or *three*.

Please do not confuse the sound of Thā' (ث) with the English /th/ in *this* and *although*, which represents the sound of another Arabic letter (ذ), known as Dhāl الذال (see Unit 4).

Notice how ث is sounded in combination with the different vowels and pronunciation symbols in the table.

Read the following letter/vowel combinations.

Supplementary vowels		Double vowels		Long vowels		Short vowels	
/thth/	ثّ	/than/	ثاً	/thā/	ثا	/tha/	ثَ
vowelless /th/	ثْ	/thun/	ثٌ	/thū/	ثو	/thu/	ثُ
/thā/	ثى	/thin/	ثٍ	/thī/	ثي	/thi/	ثِ

READ AND WRITE IT IN REAL CONTEXTS

Look at how ث is combined with other letters from previous letter groups.

Find out what letters these words are composed of and then join the combinations of letters as shown in the table.

←
Reading direction
*Practise tracing the following and copy on the line,
working from right to left.*

With long vowels

Translation	Pronunciation	Handwriting practice	Combinations	Print form
-	thā	ثا	ث ا	ثا
-	thū	ثو	ث و	ثو
-	thī	ثي	ث ي	ثي

Numbers

The first number you are going to learn is the number three and its varieties. The figure shown on the far left is Hindi since Hindi numerals are in common use in most of the Arab world (see Appendices).

	Pronunciation	Handwriting practice	Combinations	Print form
3	thalāthah	ثَلاثَة	ث ك ل ا ث َ ة	ثَلاثَة[1]
3rd	thālith	ثالِث	ث ا لِ ث	ثالِث
٣ 30	thalāthūn	ثَلاثون	ث ك ل ا ث و ن	ثَلاثون
1/3	thuluth	ثُلُث	ث ُ لُ ث	ثُلُث

Days of the week

The first day of the week you will learn is Tuesday. Notice how many times the letter Thā' is repeated in Tuesday. As ث is a sun letter, remember to pronounce it as a double consonant and assimilate the sound of ل into the word as: /ath-thulathā'/.

---

[1] The final letter (ة) is called (تاء مربوطة Tā' Marbūta, i.e. tied Tā'). It is not part of the alphabet and indicates that a word is feminine. It is usually pronounced as the letter Tā' ت /t/ when preceding another word or as /ah/ when the word is independent.

Tuesday	A(l)th-thulāthā'	_____	الثُّلَاثَاء ا ل ث ُ ل ا ث ا ء	الثُّلَاثَاء
to be firm	thabata	ثَبَتَ_____	ث َ ب َ ت	ثَبَتَ
furniture	'athāth	أثاث_____	أ ث ا ث	أثاث
my furniture	'athāthī	أثاثي_____	أ ث ا ت ي	أثاثي
to broadcast	baththa	بَثَّ_____	ب َ ثَّ	بَثَّ

The letter Nūn حَرْفُ النون

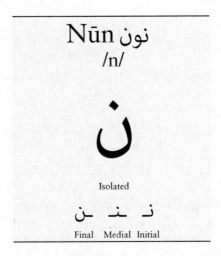

The fourth letter in this group is Nūn نون (ن), which is the twenty-fifth letter in the alphabet.

It is part of this group due to its identical basic shape with the letters ث ت ب but only in the initial and medial positions.

Its standalone shape, ن is similar to a bowl or semi-closed circle with a dot above it. In contrast to the letters Bā' ب, Tā' ت and Thā' ث, the form of Nūn goes well below the writing line.

Nūn' (ن) is a connector letter that can be joined up from both its sides with four different shapes reflecting each position (ن ـن ـنـ نـ).

Pronunciation	Joined up	Final	Medial	Initial	Isolated	Name
/n/ in nine	ننن	ـن	ـنـ	نـ	ن	نون Nūn

IN DIFFERENT CALLIGRAPHIC STYLES

This is how ن is written in different script and calligraphy styles.

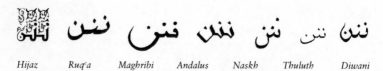

| Hijaz | Ruqʿa | Maghribi | Andalus | Naskh | Thuluth | Diwani |

HOW TO READ IT

The letter ن is transliterated and pronounced as /n/ in the word _noon_.

Notice how ن is sounded in combination with the different vowels and pronunciation symbols in the following table.

Read the following letter/vowel combinations.

Supplementary vowels		Double vowels		Long vowels		Short vowels	
/nn/	نّ	/nan/	ناً	/nā/	نا	/na/	نَ
/n'/	نْ	/nun/	نٌ	/nū/	نـو	/nu/	نُ
/nā/	نى	/nin/	نٍ	/nī/	نـي	/ni/	نِ

READ AND WRITE IT IN REAL CONTEXTS

Look at how the letter ن is combined with other letters from previous letter groups. Find out what letters these words are composed of and then join the combinations of letters as shown.

Start with the main shape, then add the dots followed by the vowels.

Translation	Pronunciation	Handwriting practice	Combinations	Print form

←
Reading direction
Practise tracing the following and copy.

With long vowels

-	nā	نا	ن ا	نا
-	nū	نو	ن و	نو
-	nī	ني	ن ي	ني

Arabic subject pronouns

Most of the subject pronouns in Arabic (I, you, he, she, etc.) are a combination of the letters ن ت أ (taught so far) and ح م ه و (to be covered later). At this stage, you will learn how to write and say: I, you (m.) and you (f.).

I	'anā	أنا	أ ن ا	أنا
you (m.)	'anta	أنتَ	أ نْ تَ	أنْتَ
you (f.)	'anti	أنتِ	أ نْ تِ	أنْتِ

Numbers

The second number you are going to learn is number two, in both ordinal and cardinal form.

٢	2	'ithnān	إثنان	إ ثْ ن ا ن	إثْنان
	2nd	a(l)th-thānī	الثَّاني	ا ل ثَّ ا ن ي	الثَّاني

son	'ibn	_____ إِبْن	إِ بْ ن	إِبْن
daughter	bint	_____ بِنْت	بِ نْ ت	بِنْت
sons or children	'abnā'	_____ أبناء	أ بْ ن ا ء	أبْناء
daughters	banāt	_____ بَنات	بَ ن ا ت	بَنات
coffee beans	bunn	_____ بُنّ	بُ نّ	بُنّ
brown (colour of coffee beans)	bunniyy	_____ بُنِّيّ	بُ نّ يّ	بُنِّيّ
name of the letter ن	nūn	_____ نون	ن و ن	نون
chopped straw	tibn	_____ تِبْن	تِ بْ ن	تِبن
milk	laban	_____ لَبَن	لَ بَ ن	لَبن
plant	nabāt	_____ نَبات	نَ ب ا ت	نَبات
plants	nabātāt	_____ نَباتات	نَ ب ا ت ا ت	نَباتات
Lebanon	lubnān	_____ لُبْنان	لُ بْ ن ا ن	لُبْنان

32

The letter Yā' حَرْفُ اليَـاء

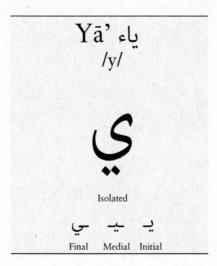

Yā' ياء
/y/

ي

Isolated

ي ـيـ ـي
Final Medial Initial

The fifth letter of this group is Yā' ياء (ي), which is the twenty-eighth and last letter in the alphabet. We are including it in this group due to the resemblance it shares with the previous letters, especially in the initial and medial form.

Yā' can serve three purposes:

1 as a long vowel representing the sound /ī/ (explained in detail in 'Vowels and pronunciation symbols');
2 as a consonant known by the sound /y/;
3 as a diphthong distinguished by the sound /ay/.

Sometimes the letter Yā' can occur twice, both as a vowel and as a consonant in the same word (e.g. Libya /lībyā/ ليبْيا).

Please bear in mind that some Arabs, Egyptian Arabs in particular, often write the letter ي as ى, i.e. by omitting the two dots both in print and handwriting. For instance نَبِيّ nabiyy, i.e. prophet, can be written as نَبِىّ, but still pronounced as nabiyy. This might leave beginner learners puzzled. To avoid such confusion, as a rule of thumb, remember that:

1 ى can only occur in the final position;
2 ى is more likely to be ي in handwritten writing.

Yā' is a connector letter that can be joined up from both its sides with four different shapes reflecting each position (ي يـ ـيـ ـي).

Pronunciation	Joined up	Final	Medial	Initial	Isolated	Name
/y/ in York	ييي	ـي	ـيـ	يـ	ي	ياء Yā'

IN DIFFERENT CALLIGRAPHIC STYLES

Hijaz   Ruqʿa   Maghribi   Andalus   Naskh   Thuluth   Diwani

HOW TO READ IT

The letter Yā' (ي) is pronounced and transliterated as /y/ in <u>Y</u>ork and <u>why</u>. Notice how ي is sounded in combination with the different vowels and pronunciation symbols in the following table.

Read the following letter/vowel combinations.

Supplementary vowels		Double vowels		Long vowels		Short vowels	
/yy/	يّ	/yan/	ياً	/yā/	يا	/ya/	يَ
vowelless /y/	يْ	/yun/	يٌّ	/yū/	يـو	/yu/	يُ
/yā/	ىـ	/yin/	يٍّ	/yī/	يـي	/yi/	يِ

34

READ AND WRITE IT IN REAL CONTEXTS

Look at how ي is combined with other letters from previous letter groups.

Find out what letters these words are composed of, then join the combinations of letters as shown in the examples.

The letter Yā' (ي) as a consonant /y/

Translation	Pronunciation	Handwriting practice	Combinations	Print form

←
Reading direction
Practise tracing the following and copy.

With long vowels

-	yā	يا	ا ي	يا
-	yū	يو	و ي	يو
-	yī	يي	ي ي	يِ

Monday	al-'ithnayn	الإثْنَين	ا ل إ ثْ نَ يْ ن	الإثْنَين
where	'ayna	أيْنَ	أ يْ نَ	أيْنَ
between	bayna	بَيْنَ	بَ يْ نَ	بَيْنَ
Laila	laylā	لَيْلى	لَ يْ ل ى	لَيْلى
he settles	yathbutu	يَثْبُت	يَ ثْ بُ تُ	يَثْبُت
he grew up	yanbutu	يَنْبُت	يَ نْ بُ تُ	يَنْبُت

البَيتُ العَرَبي

al-bayt al-ᶜarabiyy

البَيتُ ــــــــــــــــــــــــــــــ

البيت العربي, i.e. The Arabic House (Casa Arabe) is the name of a well-known institution in Spain. The script is written in a calligraphy style called *Dīwāni*, (ديواني), i.e. royal court.

Circle the letters you have learned so far. How many times do they occur in this poster?

The letter Yā' (ي) as a <u>vowel</u> (/ī/)

fig	tīn	ــــــــــــــــ	تين	ت ي ن	تين
the Nile	a(l)n-nīl	ــــــــــــــــ	النَيل	ا ل نّ ي ل	النَيل

The letter Yā' (ي) as a <u>vowel</u> and <u>consonant</u> (in the same word)

he sleeps	yabītu	ــــــــــــــــ	يَبيتُ	يَ ب ي تُ	يَبيتُ
my house	baytī	ــــــــــــــــ	بَيْتي	بَ يْ ت ي	بَيتي
Libya	lībyā	ــــــــــــــــ	ليبيا	ل ي بْ ي ا	ليبيا

36

Yā' (ي) as a multi-purpose suffix

The letter ي can serve multiple grammatical functions as a suffix when attached to the end of a word, in addition to functioning as both vowel and consonant.

These two forms have grammatical meanings in Arabic:

1 **As a possessive pronoun.** If the vowel Yā' is connected to any noun as a suffix ـِي, it is, in fact, a possessive pronoun meaning "my".

Read and practise writing the following examples:

بَيْتِي	بَيْت ←	اِبْنِي	اِبْن ←	أَبِي	أَب ←
baytī	*bayt*	*ibnī*	*'ibn*	*'abī*	*'ab*
my house	house	my son	son	my father	father

2 **As a relative adjective.** If the consonant Yā' ي is connected to any proper noun as a suffix ـِّي, you should pronounce it as a double consonant.

Read and practise writing the following examples:

بُنِّيّ	بُنّ ←	لُبْنَانِيّ	لُبْنَان ←	نَبَاتِيّ	نَبَات ←
bunniyy	*bunn*	*lubnāniyy*	*lubnān*	*nabātiyy*	*nabāt*
brown	coffee bean	Lebanese	Lebanon	vegetarian	plant

3 **As either possessive pronoun or relative adjective.**

لُبْنَانِيّ	لُبْنَانِي	لُبْنَان ←
lubnāniyy	*lubnānī*	*lubnān*
Lebanese	my Lebanon	Lebanon

ARABIC QUOTATION حِكْمَة عَرَبِيَّة

المَرْءُ مِنْ حَيْثُ يُثْبُت لا مِنْ حَيْثُ يَنْبُت

وَمِنْ حَيْثُ يوجَدُ لا مِنْ حَيْثُ يولَد

al-mar'u min ḥaythu yathbut laa min haythu yanbut
wa min haythu yuujad laa min haythu yuulad

A man belongs where he settles, and not where he grew up;
where he is now, and not where he was born

Ancient Arabic proverb

Circle the letters ب ت ث ن ي wherever you see them in the quotation.
How many times can you spot the letters ب ت ث ن ي in their different positions?

VISUAL ARABIC

Now practise recognizing the letters ب ت ث ن ي in a real and visual context:

Can you recognize the letters ب ت ث ن ي in the following images? Try reading and copying as many words as you can that contain the letters you have learnt so far.

توب شوب

توب شوب _____

This is the name of a well-known high street clothing shop.

The letter "p" does not exist in the Arabic language and so ب is used as a substitute. Can you read what the sign says?

بينو /pīno/

بينو _____

Pastry shop sign

Which letters do you recognize in this sign? Write them down in a standard Arabic script.

البَيْت

ا ل بَ يْ ت

البَيْت _____

al-bayt

House

PRINT ACCESSORIES S.A.R.L

طباعة جميع أنواع البحوث والعقود والمستندات

طباعة بحوث ورسائل الطلبة

فوطوكوبي - فاكس   عمومي - سكانير

تغليف البحوث - SPIRALE - RELIURE

الطابق الأول رقم 15ب - الهاتف: 78 04 33 039

This shop sign for print accessories lists all the services offered.

Circle all the letters you have learned so far written in different positions (isolated, initial, medial and final). How many times do they occur in this poster?

Which country does this currency note belong to?
(Hint: The country's name is written at the top of the note.)

40

SUMMARY TABLE

The following table is a summary of what you need to know about the letters ب ت ث ن ي.

Pronunciation	Joined up	Final	Medial	Initial	Isolated	Name
/b/ in *boat*	ببب	ـب	ـبـ	بـ	ب	بَاءٌ Bā
/t/ in *tea*	تتت	ـت	ـتـ	تـ	ت	تَاءٌ Tā
/th/ in *three*	ثثث	ـث	ـثـ	ثـ	ث	ثَاءٌ Thā'
/n/ in *nine*	ننن	ـن	ـنـ	نـ	ن	نونٌ Nūn
/y/ in *York*	ييي	ـي	ـيـ	يـ	ي	يَاءٌ Yā'

Test yourself

Exercise 1
Read out loud and combine the letters to form words.

ا ل ثّ ا ل ث ا ء   بَ يْ ت   تين   ت ي ن

ا ل إ ثْ نَ يْ ن   لَ بَ ن   أ ب ي

أ ث ا ت   ل ي ب ي ا   ب ا ب ا

Exercise 2
Read out loud and write the unjoined forms of the letters that make up the following words.

إبْن   إثْنان   لُبْنان

بُلْبُل   نَبات   ثُلُث

بَيْت   أنا   بِلا

Exercise 3
Transliterate the words in Exercises 1 and 2 into roman script.

Exercise 4
Place the words in Exercises 1 and 2 into the right category.

Food	Countries	Numbers	Family	Days	Miscellaneous

Exercise 5
How do you say the following relative adjectives in Arabic? Write them down.

Lebanese

Brown

Vegetarian

Exercise 6
How do you say the following in Arabic? Write them down.

My son

My house

My father

My daughter

My milk

My door

Unit **3**

Letter group no. 3

Mīm	Hā'	Tā' Marbūta	Kāf
ميم	هاء	تاء مَرْبوطَة	كاف
/m/	/h/	/t/	/k/

م	ه ه	ة/ة	ك
Isolated	Isolated		Isolated

م ـمـ مـ	ه ـهـ هـ	ة/ـة	ك ـكـ كـ
Final Medial Initial	Final Medial Initial	Final	Final Medial Initial

In this unit you will learn
- *how to write and join the letters* م ك ه ة
- *how to read and recognize the letters in real contexts in a variety of script styles*
- *new and commonly used words*

The third letter group is very mixed and consists of three dissimilar letters with unique and independent skeleton shapes:

1 Mīm ميم (م)
2 Hā' هاء (ه)
3 Kāf كاف (ك).

Plus the tied-up Tā'/Tā' Marbūta تاء مربوطة (a non-alphabetical letter) (ة /ـة).

Letter group no. 3 in a nutshell

Pronun-ciation	Joined up	Final	Medial	Initial	Isolated	Name	
/m/ in mine	ممم	ـم	ـمـ	مـ	م	ميم	Mīm
/k/ in kayak	ككك	ـك	ـكـ	كـ	ك	كاف	Kāf
/h/ in him	ههه	ه/ـه	ـهـ	هـ	ه	هاء	Hā'
/t/	-	ة/ـة	-	-	-	تاء مَرْبوطَة	tied-up Tā' Tā' Marbūta

The letter Mīm حَرْفُ الميم

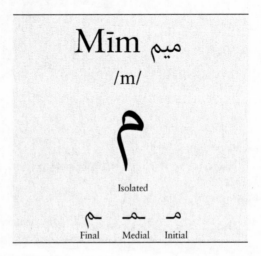

Mīm ميم

/m/

م

Isolated

ـم ـمـ مـ

Final Medial Initial

The first letter of this group is letter Mīm ميم (م), which is the twenty-fourth letter in the Arabic alphabet.

م is a connector letter with four different shapes (م ممم) (see table).

The main feature of this letter is its distinct core shape similar to a round bead that does not vary too much when connected to other letters. Just bear in mind that:

- The bead of the initial and medial forms are written above the line (مـ ـمـ).
- While in the final form, the tail of the letter م goes below the line with a vertical stroke.

Pronunciation	Joined up	Final	Medial	Initial	Isolated	Name
/m/ in mine	ممم	ـم	ـمـ	مـ	م	ميم Mīm

HOW TO WRITE IT

Skeleton shape

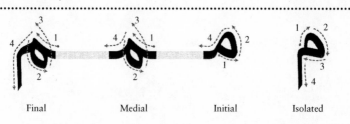

| Final | Medial | Initial | Isolated |

In the following activity, you will learn how to write the core skeleton shape of the letter م in the four different positions. Then you will practise writing all these positions connected in one imaginary word.

Following the diagram of the skeleton shape, practise tracing the following and copy.

←

م م م   م

ـمـ ـمـ ـمـ   ـم

IN DIFFERENT CALLIGRAPHIC STYLES

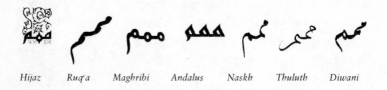

| Hijaz | Ruq'a | Maghribi | Andalus | Naskh | Thuluth | Diwani |

HOW TO READ IT

The letter م is transliterated and pronounced as /m/ as in the word
<u>*mime*</u>.

Notice how م is sounded in combination with the different vowels
and pronunciation symbols in the table.

*Read the following letter/vowel combinations, working from
right to left.*

Supplementary vowels		Double vowels		Long vowels		Short vowels	
/mm/	مّ	/man/	مًا	/mā/	ما	/ma/	مَ
vowelless /m/	مْ	/mun/	مٌّ	/mū/	مو	/mu/	مُ
/mā/	مى	/min/	مٍ	/mī/	مي	/mi/	مِ

READ AND WRITE IT IN REAL CONTEXTS

Look at how م is combined with other letters from the previous letter groups.

Find out what letters these words are composed of, then join the combinations of letters as shown.

Translation	Pronun-ciation	Handwriting practice	Combinations	Print form

←
Reading direction
Practise tracing the following and copy.

With long vowels

-	mā	ما	م ا	ما
-	mū	مو	م و	مو
-	mī	مي	م ي	مي

what	mā	ما	م ا	ما
when (question noun)	matā	مَتى	مَ ت ى	مَتى
who	man	مَنْ	مَ نْ	مَنْ
from	min	مِنْ	مِ نْ	مِنْ
in front of	'amāma	أمامَ	أ م ا مَ	أَمامَ
not	lam	لَمْ	لَ مْ	لَمْ
when, since	lammā	لَمّا	لَ مّ ا	لَمّا

QUICK VOCAB

Family members

So far you have learned that "father" in Arabic is أب /'ab/ (formal) or بابا /bābā/ (informal).

Another important family member you will learn here is the formal and informal Arabic for "mother".

Mother (formal)	'umm	ـــــــــ أمّ	أ مّ	أمّ
My mother	'ummī	ـــــــــ أمّي	أ مّ ي	أمّي
Mum (informal)	māmā	ـــــــــ ماما	م ا م ا	ماما

Arabic subject pronouns

So far you have learned the following three subject pronouns: أنا أَنْتِ أَنْتَ.

Match these pronouns to their transliteration ('anti, 'anā, 'anta) and translation (you (f.), you (m.), I).

Next, you will learn how to read and write three more subject pronouns: you (m. pl.), you (f. pl.) and you (dual).

you (m. pl.)	'antum	ـــــــــ أنْتُم	أ نْ تُ م	أنْتم
you (f. pl.)	'antunna	ـــــــــ أنْتُنَّ	أ نْ تُ نَّ	أنْتُنَّ
you (dual)	'antumā	ـــــــــ أنْتُما	أ نْ تُ م ا	أنْتُما

Numbers

The next number you are going to learn is the number eight, and its varieties.

	8	thamāniyah	ـــــــــ ثَمانِية	ثَ م ا نِ يَ ة	ثَمانِية
	8th	a(l)th-thāmin/ah	ـــــــــ التَّامِن	ا ل ثّ ا م ن	التَّامِن/ة
٨	80	thamānūn	ـــــــــ ثَمانون	ثَ م ا ن و ن	ثَمانون
	1/8	thumun	ـــــــــ ثُمن	ثُ مُ ن	ثُمن

48

The number 100 has two different spellings: مِئَة or مائة (the latter is pronounced exactly the same as /mi'ah/ but with a silent Alif ١.

١٠٠	100	mi'ah	مِئَة مائة	م ئ ة م ا ئ ة	مِئَة / مائة

Germany	'almāniyā		أَلْمانيا	أ ل م ا ن ي ا	أَلْمانِيا
Melilla[1]	malīlyah		مَلِيلْية	م ل ي لْ يَ ة	مَلِيلْية
Al Manamah[2]	al-manāmah		المَنامَة	ا ل مَ ن ا مَ ة	المَنامَة
lemon	laymūn		لَيْمون	لَ يْ م و ن	لَيْمون
water	mā'		ماء	م ا ء	ماء
money	māl		مال	م ا ل	مال
excellent	tamām		تَمام	تَ م ا م	تَمام

اليَمَن / اليَمَنِيّة

ا ل يَ مَ نِ / ا ل يَ مَ نِ يَّ ة

اليَمَن / اليَمَنِيّة

al-yaman/-iyyah
Yemen/Yemeni Airline

---

[1]Melilla is a city located in Morocco.

[2]Al Manamah is the capital and largest city in Bahrain.

Nicknames

It is common custom among Arabs and Muslims alike to call a man or woman with the name of their first-born son or daughter. The father is nicknamed 'abū (أَبُو ...) "father of (child's name)" and the mother as 'umm (أُمّ ...) "mother of (child's name)". So, for instance, the father and mother of Lubna (لُبْنى) are nicknamed as:

أُمّ لُبْنى	أَبُو لُبْنى
أم لُبْنى	أبو لُبْنى

'umm lubna
mother of Lubna

'abū lubna
father of Lubna

So, next time you meet an Arab or Muslim, you can easily work out their nickname by finding out the name of their first child.

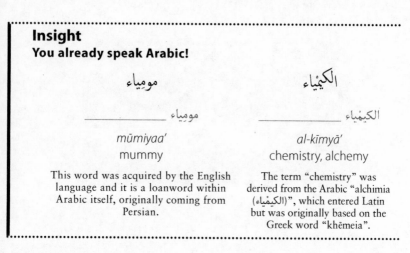

Insight
You already speak Arabic!

مومِياء	الكيمْياء
مومِياء	الكيمْياء

mūmiyaa'
mummy

al-kīmyā'
chemistry, alchemy

This word was acquired by the English language and it is a loanword within Arabic itself, originally coming from Persian.

The term "chemistry" was derived from the Arabic "alchimia (الكيمْياء)", which entered Latin but was originally based on the Greek word "khēmeia".

Notice where the Hamza sign (ء) is written in these two examples: resting on the line, level with the other letters.

The letter Hā' حَرْفُ الهاء

Hā' هاء
/h/

ه

Isolated

ـه | ـهـ | هـ
Final | Medial | Initial

The second of this group is Hā' هاء (ه), which is the twenty-sixth letter in the Arabic alphabet. It is a connector letter with four shapes and it does not share its skeleton shape with any other letters.

ه is considered a complicated letter to write and pronounce among students of Arabic. But do not worry: it is not impossible to master. With persistent writing practise and attentive listening, you will easily learn to write and pronounce it fluently like an Arab.

Unlike other letters, its shape changes completely according to its position in the word (see table).

Pronunciation	Joined up	Final	Medial	Initial	Isolated	Name
"h" in him (voiced counterpart of Haa' ح)	ههه	ـه / ه	ـهـ or ـ	ه	ه	هاء Hā'

Skeleton shape

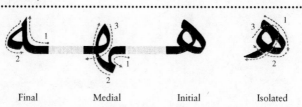

| Final | Medial | Initial | Isolated |

In the following activity, you will learn how to write the letter (ه) in the four different positions: isolated, initial, medial (two different forms: print and handwritten) and final (two different forms: connected and non-connected).

Then you will practise writing all the positions connected in one imaginary word.

Following the diagram of the skeleton shape, practise tracing the following and copy on the line, working from right to left.

ه in the final position, in two forms:

1 when attached to connecting letters;
2 when attached to non-connecting letters.

IN DIFFERENT CALLIGRAPHIC STYLES

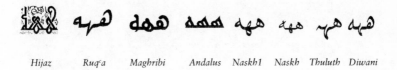

| Hijaz | Ruq'a | Maghribi | Andalus | Naskh1 | Naskh | Thuluth | Diwani |

HOW TO READ IT

The letter Hā' (ه) is transliterated as /h/ and pronounced like the English /h/ in *him* and *her*.

The nearest sound to Hā' (ه) is that of Ḥa' ح /ḥ/ (see Unit 5). But do not confuse the two sounds Hā' (ه) and Ḥa' ح. Pay attention to how you pronounce the following similar sounding examples:

| /fahm/ understanding | فَهْم | vs | فَحْم | /faḥm/ coal |

Notice how ه is sounded in combination with the different vowels and pronunciation symbols in the table.

Read the following letter/vowel combinations.

Supplementary vowels		Double vowels		Long vowels		Short vowels	
/hh/	هّ	/han/	هًا	/hā/	ها	/ha/	هَ
vowelless /h/	هْ	/hun/	هٌ	/hū/	هو	/hu/	هُ
/hā/	هى	/hin/	هٍ	/hī/	هي	/hi/	هِ

READ AND WRITE IT IN REAL CONTEXTS

Look at how ه is combined with other letters from the previous letter groups.

Find out what letters these words are composed of, then join the combinations of letters as shown.

Translation	Pronunciation	Handwriting practice	Combinations	Print form

←
Reading direction
Practise tracing the following and copy.

With long vowels

-	hā	ـــــــــــــــ ها	ه ا	ها
-	hū	ـــــــــــــــ هو	ه و	هو
-	hī	ـــــــــــــــ هي	ه ي	هي

Arabic subject pronouns

So far you have learned all the subject pronouns in the first person (أنا /'anā'/ I) and the second person (أنْتَ /'anta'/ you (m.), أنْتِ /'anti'/ you (f.), etc.). At this stage, you will learn how to read and write remaining subject pronouns, i.e. the third person: he, she, they (m.), (f.) and dual.

he	huwa	ـــــــــــــــ هُوَ	هُ وَ	هُوَ
she	hiya	ـــــــــــــــ هِيَ	هِ يَ	هِيَ
they (m.)	hum	ـــــــــــــــ هُمْ	هُ مْ	هُمْ
they (f.)	hunna	ـــــــــــــــ هُنَّ	هُ نَّ	هُنَّ
they (dual)	humā	ـــــــــــــــ هُما	هُ م ا	هُما

Arabic possessive pronouns

Possessive pronouns are words such as my, your, his, her, etc. So far, you have learned one possessive pronoun suffix ـِي, i.e. my. Here, you will learn how to read and write the Arabic equivalents of his, her and their in (m.), (f.) and dual.

his	-hu	ـهُ-	هُ ـ	ـهُ-
her	-hā	ـها-	ا هـ ـ	ـها-
their (m.)	-hum	ـهُمْ-	مْ هُ ـ	ـهُمْ-
their (f.)	-hunna	ـهُنَّ-	نَّ هُ ـ	ـهُنَّ-
their (dual)	-humā	ـهُما-	ا مُ هُ ـ	ـهُما-

For instance, if we use the possessive pronoun suffixes above with the word بَيْت bayt (house), you will get the following combinations:

Read aloud and practise writing the following.

بَيْتُهُما	بَيْتُهُنَّ	بَيْتُهُمْ	بَيْتُها	بَيْتُهُ	بَيْت ←
baytuhumā	*baytuhunna*	*baytuhum*	*baytuhā*	*baytuhu*	*bayt*
their house (dual)	their house (f. pl.)	their house (m. pl.)	her house	his house	house

Question nouns

Interrogative noun to ask yes or no questions e.g. Are you…?	hal	هَلْ لْ هَ هَلْ

Examples

Are you from Lebanon?	هَلْ أَنْتَ مِنَ لُبْنان؟ هَلْ أَنْتَ مِنَ لُبْنان؟
Is she Yemeni?	هَلْ هِيَ يَمَنِيَّة؟ هَلْ هِيَ يَمَنِيَّة؟

Insight: God in Arabic

god (general meaning)   'ilāh   _____   إِلَـٰهُ   إِ لَ ـ هـ   إله[1]

God   allāh   _____   ٱللَّهُ   ا ل ل ه   الله

Although it is commonly known that the word Allah is widely used by Muslims to refer to God, Arabic speakers of other Abrahamic faiths including Jews and Christians also use it for the same purpose. For instance, Christians say:

الله الروح القُدْس	الله الإبْن	الله الأَب
الله الروح القُدْس	الله الإبْن	الله الأَب
_____	_____	_____
Allāh a(l)r-rūḥ al-quds	Allāh al-'ibn	Allāh al-'ab
God the Holy Spirit	God the Son	God the Father

In fact, the word Allah is the most frequently repeated proper noun in the Holy Qur'an (around 2704 times)[2]. There are many usages of the word الله in everyday spoken Arabic and Islamic discourse, to mention a few:

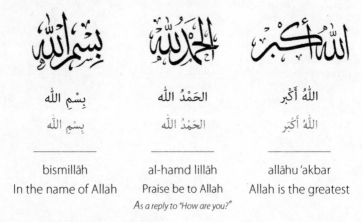

بِسْمِ الله	الحَمْدُ الله	اللهُ أَكْبَر
بِسْمِ الله	الحَمْدُ الله	اللهُ أَكْبَر
_____	_____	_____
bismillāh	al-hamd lillāh	allāhu 'akbar
In the name of Allah	Praise be to Allah	Allah is the greatest
	As a reply to "How are you?"	

---

[1]Notice the tiny letter Alif (ا) just after the letter ل and above the Shaddah sign (ـّ). This is called hidden or dagger Alif and should be treated as a long vowel when reading the word.

[2]The most frequently used word in the Qur'an above the word الله is مِن min, i.e. from mentioned 3226 times (corpus.quran.com).

56

There is no God but Allah, and Mohammad is Allah's messenger
Lā ílāha illallāh muhammad rasūlu llah

This expression is referred to as "الشهادة a(l)sh-shahaadah," i.e.
Islamic testimony of faith and regarded as the most memorized
expression among Muslims. The recitation of this testimony is
considered as the most important of the five pillars of Islam.

The declaration reads لا إلـه إلاَّ الله مُحَمَّد رَسولُ الله.

IN DIFFERENT CALLIGRAPHIC STYLES

Here are a few examples of the word Allah الله written in different
script and calligraphy styles.

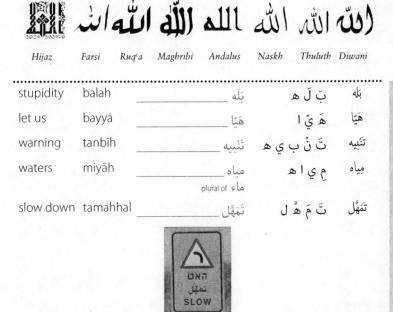

	Hijaz	Farsi	Ruq'a	Maghribi	Andalus	Naskh	Thuluth	Diwani

stupidity	balah		بَلَه	هـ لَ ـب	بَله
let us	bayyā		هَيَّا	هَ يِّ ا	هَيَّا
warning	tanbīh		تَنْبيه	تَ نْ ب ي هـ	تَنْبيه
waters	miyāh		مياه	مِ ي ا هـ	مِياه
			plural of مَأْء		
slow down	tamahhal		تَمَهَّل	تَ مَ هَّ ل	تَمَهَّل

QUICK VOCAB

Tā' Marbūta تاء مَربوطة
/t/

ة/ـة

Final position only

This is a supplementary letter and not considered part of the Arabic alphabet. It appears only in word final positions and it is called Tā' Marbūta تاء مربوطة, i.e tied Tā', to distinguish it from the normal open-shaped Tā' تاء مفتوحة (ت) (see Unit 2).

In the Arabic language, there is no equivalent for "it" as usually used for animals and inanimate objects. Like many other European languages, Arabic has two genders: masculine and feminine.

ة/ـة has a unique grammatical function indicating, in most cases, a feminine ending: however, there are a few exceptions and not all feminine nouns have the feminine ending ة/ـة.

The shape of ة/ـة is similar to that of ه in final forms ـه/ه, but distinguished with two dots above.

Pronun- ciation	Joined up	Final	Medial	Initial	Isolated	Name	
t	-	ة/ـة	-	-	-	تاء مَرْبوطَة	Tā' Marbūta Tied- up Tā'

HOW TO WRITE IT

ة/ـة is written exactly the same way as the letter ه in the final position (ـه/ه).

In this activity, you will learn how to write the core shape of the feminine ending (ة) in two forms:

1 when attached to connecting letters.

2 when following non-connecting letters.

Practise tracing the following and copy.

ـة	ـة ـة ـة		
ة	ة ة ة		

HOW TO READ IT

When you read the following examples, which all end with ة/ـة, you will notice that the letter preceding ة/ـة carries the vowel Fatha (ـَ), which is always pronounced. In spoken Arabic, however, the ة/ـة is not normally pronounced when the word is independent and thus pronounced as /ah/.

As a rule of thumb, remember that in most cases when a word ends with a Fatha (ـَ) you can assume that it is feminine carrying ة/ـة.

Study and read the following examples:

قَناة	وَرْدَة	لَيْمونَة	ثَمانِيَة	ثَلاثَة	اِبْنَة
qanāh	wardah	laymūnah	thamāniyah	thalāthah	ibnah
channel	rose				

Can you figure out the English meaning of the other feminine words?

When ة/ـة is connected to any following letter, it is treated exactly like the normal Tā' (ت), both in writing and pronunciation.

my lemon	laymūnatī	_____	لَيْمونَتي ← ي + لَيْمونَة
my daughter	'ibnatī	_____	اِبْنَتي ← ي + اِبْنَة

Scan this wall sign for the letter ة/ـة and circle the occurences. How many are there?

_____

The letter Kāf حَرْفُ الكاف

كاف Kāf
/k/

كـ

Isolated

كـ   ـكـ   ك

Final   Medial   Initial

The last letter of this group is letter Kāf كاف (ك), which is the twenty-second letter in the Arabic alphabet. It is a connector letter with four shapes and it does not share its skeleton shape with any other letters.

ك has a unique and independent shape. The core shape of the isolated and final position is similar to Lām, but written along the line and carrying in the middle a miniature Kāf (ك) (in initial position), which also resembles the hamza sign (ء).

Pronunciation	Joined up	Final	Medial	Initial	Isolated	Name
/k/ in kayak	ككك	ـك	ـكـ	كـ	ك	كاف Kāf

HOW TO WRITE IT

Skeleton shape

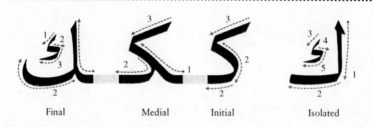

Final   Medial   Initial   Isolated

In the following activity, you will learn how to write the core skeleton shape of the letter ك in the four different positions. Then you will practise writing all these positions connected in one imaginary word.

Following the skeleton shape diagram, start with the main shape, and then add the Hamza-shaped symbol in the middle above the letter.

Practise tracing the following and copy.

$\leftarrow$

_____ ك ك ك   كـ

_____ ـكـ ـكـ ـكـ   ـكـ

_____ ـك ـك ـك   ـك

ك   ك ك ك _____

ككك   ككك ككك ككك _____

....

IN DIFFERENT CALLIGRAPHIC STYLES

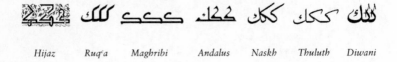

| Hijaz | Ruq'a | Maghribi | Andalus | Naskh | Thuluth | Diwani |

HOW TO READ IT

ك is transliterated and pronounced as /k/ in the English word _kayak_.

Notice how ك is sounded in combination with the different vowels and pronunciation symbols in the table.

Read the following letter/vowel combinations.

Supplementary vowels		Double vowels		Long vowels		Short vowels	
/kk/	كْ	/kan/	كًا	/kā/	كا	/ka/	كَ
vowelless /k/	كْ	/kun/	كٌ	/kū/	كو	/ku/	كُ
/kā/	كى	/kin/	كٍ	/kī/	كي	/ki/	كِ

....

READ AND WRITE IT IN REAL CONTEXTS

Look at how ك is combined with other letters from the previous letter groups.

Find out what letters these words are composed of, then join the combinations of letters as shown.

←
Reading direction
Practise tracing the following and copy.

With long vowels

-	kā	_____ كَا	كـ ا	كَا
-	kū	_____ كو	كـ و	كو
-	kī	_____ كي	كـ ي	كي

how much/many	kam	_____ كَمْ	كَ مْ	كَمْ
every, all	kull	_____ كُل	كُ ل	كل
possible	mumkin	_____ مُمْكِن	مُ مْ كِ ن	مُمكِن
mecca	makkah	_____ مَكَّة	مَ كَّ ة	مَكَّة
kilo	kīlū	_____ كيلو	كـ ي ل و	كيلو
dog	kalb	_____ كَلْب	كَ لْ ب	كَلْب
bank	bank	_____ بَنْك	بَ نْ ك	بَنْك
speech	kalām	_____ كلام	كَ ل ا م	كلام
word	kalimah	_____ كَلِمَة	كَ لِ مَ ة	كَلِمَة
king/queen	malik/ah	_____ مَلِك/ة	مَ لِ كـ /ة	مَلِك/ة

QUICK VOCAB

Arabic possessive pronouns

So far, you have learned the possessive pronoun suffix ي, i.e. my, and then all the ones for the third person (ـه-his, ـها- her, etc.).

Here, you will learn to read and write the Arabic equivalents of "your" in both genders, in plural and dual form.

your (m.)	-ka	_____	ـكَ-	كَ	ـكَ
your (f.)	-ki	_____	ـكِ-	ـكِ	كِ
your (m. pl.)	-kum	_____	ـكُمْ-	مْ كُ ـ	كُمْ
your (f. pl.)	-kunna	_____	ـكُنَّ-	كُ ـ نَّ	كُنَّ
your (dual)	-kumā	_____	ـكُما-	كُ ـ ما ا	كُما

For instance, if we use these possessive pronoun suffixes with the word بيت (bayt) again, you will get the following combinations:

بَيْتُكُما	بَيْتُكُنَّ	بَيْتُكُم	بَيْتُكِ	بَيْتُكَ	بَيْت ←
baytukumā	*bay-tukunna*	*bay-tukum*	*baytuki*	*baytuka*	*bayt*
your house (dual)	your house (f. pl.)	their house (m. pl.)	your house (f.)	your house (m.)	house

VISUAL ARABIC

Foreign words in Arabic

To improve your visual learning of Arabic, have a look at the following images and challenge yourself: can you read the foreign names within them?

Can you identify the letters (ة/ـة هـ م كـ) in the following foreign words signs?

Read aloud and copy in the space provided.

كوكاكولا

ك و ك ا ك و ل ا

كوكاكولا _____

Circle the letters you have learnt so far: ا ب ت ن ي ك م ه.

(Hint: The letter س/ـس is pronounced as /s/ in *seen*.)

كريسبي كريم

ك و ك ا ك و ل ا

كريسبي كريم _____

Circle the letter ك in the sign.

(Hint: The letter س/ـس is pronounced as /s/ in *seen*.)

ايكيا

ا ي ك ي ا

ايكيا _____

(Hint: The letter Yā' (ي) occurs twice in the sign. Read it as a consonant and not as a vowel.)

كنتاكي

ك ن ت ا ك ي

كنتاكي _____

Read the second word out loud.

إلكترونيك _____ طوكيو _____

The name of this shop sign is all foreign transcribed in Arabic. Circle the letter ك in the sign. How many times does it occur?

(Hint: The letter ط is pronounced as Spanish /t/ in *patatas*.)

The signs in the pictures are: Coca-Cola, Crispy Crème, Ikea, Kentucky Chicken and Electronic Tokyo.

66

ARABIC QUOTATION حِكْمَة عَرَبِيَّة

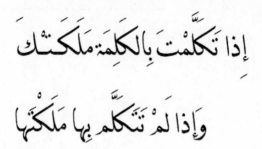

إِذَا تَكَلَّمْتَ بِالكَلِمَةِ مَلَكَتْكَ

وَإِذَا لَمْ تَتَكَلَّمْ بِهَا مَلَكْتَهَا

idhā takallamta bi al kalimah malakatka wa 'idhā lam tatakllam bihā malakthā

If you speak the word it shall own you, and if you don't you shall own it

Arabic proverb

Circle the letters ة ك ه م wherever you see them in the quotation. How many times can you spot the letters ة ك ه م in their different positions?

Do you recognize any familiar words in the quotation that you have learned so far?

SUMMARY TABLE

The following table is a summary of what you need to know about the letters ك م ه and the additional letter ـة/ة.

Pronunciation	Joined up	Final	Medial	Initial	Isolated		Name
/m/ in mine	ممم	ـم/ـم	ـمـ	مـ	م	ميم	Mīm
/k/ in kayak	ككك	ك	ـكـ	كـ	ك	كاف	Kāf
/h/ in him	ههه	ـه/ه	ـهـ	هـ	ه	هاء	Hā'
/t/	-	ـة/ة	-	-	-	تاء مَرْبوطَة	Tied-up Tā' Tā' Marbūtā

Test yourself

Exercise 1
Read out loud and combine the letters to form words.

مَ ء ا   ماء   ثَ م ا نِ يَ ة   لَ يْ م و ن

ا ل لَ ه   كِ ت ا ب   مَ كَّ ة

Exercise 2
Read out loud and write the unjoined forms of the letters that
make up the following words.

ثَمانون   المَنامَة   م ا م ا   ماما

اليَمَن   الكيمْياء   أمامَ

Exercise 3
Transliterate the words in Exercises 1 and 2 into roman script.

Exercise 4
Place the words in Exercises 1 and 2 into the right category.

Food	Countries	Cities	Family	Religious	Numbers	Miscellaneous

Exercise 5
Read the following expressions and translate into English.

هُوَ يَمَنِيّ.هُوَ مِنَ اليَمَن   مِنْ أَيْنَ أَنْتَ؟

الحَمْدُ لله   مَنْ أَنْتِ؟

الله الإبن   هِيَ أَلْمانِيَّة. هِيَ مِنْ أَلْمانِيا

الله الأب   أُمِّي مِنْ لِيبْيا

68

Exercise 6
Translate the following expressions into Arabic.

I am Libyan. I am from Libya

I am German. I am from Germany

Where are you (m. pl.) from?

Who are you (m.)?

Are you (f.) Lebanese? Is she German?

Are you (m. pl.) Yemeni?

Exercise 7
Fill in the gaps with the correct translations and transliterations.

كِتابُكُما	كِتابُكُم	كِتابُكَ	← كِتاب
kitābukumā	kitābukum	kitābuka	kitāb
	your	your	
	book	book	
	(f. pl.)	(f.)	

Exercise 8
How do we say and write the following nicknames in Arabic?

Father of Mary

Mother of Mary

Unit 4

Letter group no. 4: non-connectors (part I)

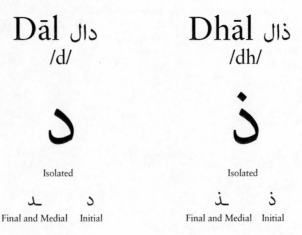

Dāl دال
/d/

 د

Isolated

ـد   د

Final and Medial   Initial

Dhāl ذال
/dh/

ذ

Isolated

ـذ   ذ

Final and Medial   Initial

In this unit you will learn
- *how to write and join the non-connector letters ذ د*
- *how to read and recognize these letters in real contexts and in a variety of script styles*
- *new and commonly used vocabulary using these letters*

In the Arabic alphabet, there are 22 connector letters and six non-connectors. The non-connector letters are Alif (ا), Dāl (د), Dhāl (ذ), Rāy (ر), Zāy (ز) and Wāw (و).

Connecting letters join both the preceding and the following letters, while non-connecting letters can be joined to the preceding letters but never to any following letters. As a result, they only have two different positions.

Their shape does not change no matter what their position, except that they need to be connected to the preceding letter cursively.

When writing non-connecting letters, make sure you leave a small gap between the letters. Study the following examples.

QUICK VOCAB

or	'aw	أ وْ	أوْ
if	'idhā	إ ذ ا	إذا
house	dār	د ا ر	دار
river	wād	و ا د	واد
roses	ward	وَ زْ د	وَرْد
to visit	zāra	ز ا رَ	زارَ
visit (imperative verb)	zur	زُ رْ	زُرْ
role	dawr	دَ وْ ر	دَوْر
rice	'aruzz	أ رُ ز	أُرْز
they increased (in number)	izdādū	ا ز د ا د و	ازدادو
ministers	wuzarā'	وُ زَ ر ا ء	وُزراء
visit (pl.)	zūrū	ز و ر و	زورو

The two letters ذ د of this group have already been introduced in the "Vowels and pronunciation symbols" section purposely to help you learn how to pronounce the different vowels and pronunciation symbols in Arabic.

They are part of the non-connectors and only have two different positions.

Letter group no. 4 in a nutshell

Pronunciation	Joined up	Final and Medial	Initial and Isolated	Name
/d/ in dice	n/a	ـد	د	دال Dāl
/dh/ in though	n/a	ـذ	ذ	ذال Dhāl

HOW TO WRITE IT

Skeleton shape

Medial and Final   Isolated and Initial

In the following activity, you will learn how to write the core skeleton shape of the letters ذ د in the four different positions. Then you will practise writing all these positions connected in one imaginary word.

Practise tracing the following and copy.

←

د د د   د

ـد ـد ـد   ـد

ددد ددد ددد   ددد

Now, repeat the same writing exercise for the letter ذ.

IN DIFFERENT CALLIGRAPHIC STYLES

This is how د is written in different script and calligraphy styles. The letter ذ will look exactly the same, with the exception of a dot above it.

Hijaz	Ruqʿa	Maghribi	Andalus	Naskh	Thuluth	Diwani

The letter Dāl حَرْفُ الدَّال

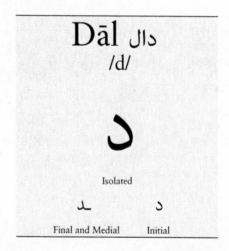

Dāl دال
/d/

 د
Isolated

ـد   د
Final and Medial   Initial

The first letter of this group is Dāl دال (د), which is the eighteenth letter in the Arabic alphabet.

د is a non-connector letter with only two different shapes (ـد د) (see table).

Pronunciation	Joined up	Final and Medial	Initial and Isolated	Name
/d/ in dice	د د د	ـد	د	دال Dāl

HOW TO READ IT

The letter Dāl دال (د) is transliterated and pronounced as frontal /d/ in the word dice. Notice how د is sounded in combination with the different vowels and pronunciation symbols in the table.

Read the following letter/vowel combinations.

Supplementary vowels		Double vowels		Long vowels		Short vowels	
/d-d/	دْ	/dan/	دًا	/dā/	دا	/da/	دَ
vowelless /d/	دْ	/dun/	دٌ	/dū/	دو	/du/	دُ
/dā/	دى	/din/	دٍ	/dī/	دي	/di/	دِ

READ AND WRITE IT IN REAL CONTEXTS

Look at how د is combined with other letters from the previous letter groups.

Find out what letters these words are composed of, join the combinations of letters as shown here, then compare how the script is written in print and handwritten form.

Start with the main shape, then add the dots followed by the vowels.

Translation	Pronunciation	Handwriting practice	Combinations	Print form
		←		

Reading direction
Practise tracing the following and copy.

With long vowels

-	dā	_____ دا	د ا	دا
-	dū	_____ دو	د و	دو
-	dī	_____ دي	د ي	دي

sure, absolutely	'akīd	_____ أكيد	أ ك ي د	أكيد
author	'adīb	_____ أَديب	أ د ي ب	أَديب
hand	yad	_____ يَد	يَ د	يَد
to begin	bada'a	_____ بَدأ	بَ دَ أ	بَدأ
beginning	bidāyah	_____ بِداية	ب د ا يَ ة	بِداية
literature	'adab	_____ أدَب	أ دَ ب	أدَب
director, manager	mudīr	_____ مُدير	مُ د ي ر	مُدير
always	dāiman	_____ دائماً	د ا ئِ م اً	دائماً
Dubai	dubai	_____ دُبَي	دُ بَ ي	دُبَي
city	madīnah	_____ مَدينة	م د ي ن ة	مَدينة

City of Madīnah (Saudi Arabia) al-madīnah المَدينة

Letter group no. 4 75

The letter Dhāl حَرْفُ الذّال

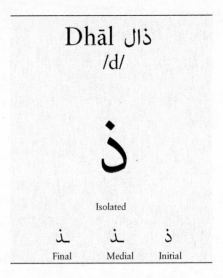

Dhāl ذال
/d/

ذ

Isolated

ذـ ـذـ ذ

Final   Medial   Initial

Another non-connector letter is Dhāl ذال (ذ), which is the nineteenth letter in the Arabic alphabet.

ذ is a non-connector letter with only two different shapes (ـذ ذ) (see table).

Pronunciation	Joined up	Final and Medial	Initial and Isolated	Name
/dh/ in though	ذ ذ ذ	ـذ	ذ	ذال Dhāl

HOW TO READ IT

The letter Dhāl (ذ) is transliterated and pronounced as /dh/ as in the words _this_, _that_ and _though_.

Notice how ذ is sounded in combination with the different vowels and pronunciation symbols in the table.

Read the following letter/vowel combinations.

Supplementary vowels		Double vowels		Long vowels		Short vowels	
/dh-dh/	ذّ	/dhan/	اذً	/dhā/	اذ	/dha/	ذَ
vowelless /dh/	ذْ	/dhun/	ذٌ	/dhū/	ذو	/dhu/	ذُ
/dhā/	ذى	/dhin/	ذٍ	/dhī/	ذي	/dhi/	ذِ

READ AND WRITE IT IN REAL CONTEXTS

Look at how ذ is combined with other letters from the previous letter groups.

Find out what letters these words are composed of, join the combinations of letters as shown, then compare how the script is written in print and handwritten form.

Start with the main shape first, then add the dots followed by the vowels.

Translation	Pronunciation	Handwriting practice	Combinations	Print form

←
Reading direction
Practise tracing the following and copy.

With long vowels

-	dhā	_____ذا	ا ذ	ذا
-	dhū	_____ذو	ذ و	ذو
-	dhī	_____ذي	ذ ي	ذي

This and that: Arabic demonstrative pronouns

this (m.)	hādhā	_____هذا	ه ـ ذ ا	هـٰذا[1]
this (f.)	hādhihi	_____هذه	ه ـ ذ ه	هـٰذِه
that	dhālika	_____ذلك	ذ ـ ل ك	ذلك

---

[1]Notice that both these nouns have a hidden or dagger Alif which should be treated as a normal vowel Alif when pronouncing the word.

what	mādhā	_____ ماذا	م ا ذ ا	ماذا
Islamic leader (often of a mosque or the community)	'imām	_____ إمام	إ م ا م	إمام
religion	dīn	_____ دين	د ي ن	دين
debt	dayn	_____ دَين	دَ يْ ن	دَيْن
life	dunyā	_____ دُنْيا	دُ نْ ي ا	دُنْيا
Islamic call to prayer	'adhān	_____ أذان	أ ذ ا ن	أذان
minaret	manārah	_____ مَنارَة	مَ ن ا رَ ة	مَنارَة
self	dhāt	_____ ذات	ذ ا ت	ذات
to melt	dhāba	_____ ذابَ	ذ ا بَ	ذابَ
to go (v.)	dhahaba	_____ ذَهَب	ذَ هَ بَ	ذَهَب
gold (n.)	dhahab	_____ ذَهَب	ذَ هَ ب	ذَهَب
fly (insect)	dhubābah	_____ ذُبابة	ذُ ب ا بَ ة	ذُبابة
delicious	ladhīdh	_____ لَذيذ	لَ ذ ي ذ	لَذيذ
intelligent	dhakiyy	_____ ذَكِيّ	ذَ كِ يّ	ذَكِيّ
melted	dhā'ib	_____ ذائِب	ذ ا ئِ ب	ذائِب
aubergine	bādhinjān	_____ باذِنْجان	ب ا ذِ نْ ج ا ن	باذِنْجان

ARABIC QUOTATION حِكْمَة عَرَبِيَّة

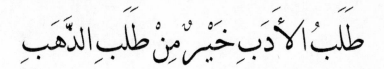

طَلَبُ الْأَدَبِ خَيْرٌ مِنْ طَلَبِ الذَّهَبِ

ṭalabu al-'yadab khayrun min ṭalabi a(l)dh-dhahab

Seeking education is better than searching for gold

Arabic proverb

Circle the letters ذ د wherever you see them in the quotation.
Do you recognize in the quotation any familiar words that
you have learned so far?

SUMMARY TABLE

The following table is a summary of what you need to know about
the letters ذ د.

Pronunciation	Joined up	Final and Medial	Initial and Isolated	Name
/d/ in dice	د د د	ـد	د	دال Dāl
/dh/ in though	ذ ذ ذ	ـذ	ذ	ذال Dhāl

Test yourself

Exercise 1
Read out loud and combine the letters to form words.

ذ ـ ل ك   أ ك ي د   هـ ذا   هـ ذا

ذ ب ا بَ ة   هـ ـ ذِ ه   د ي ن

Exercise 2
Read out loud and write the unjoined forms of the letters that make up the following words.

أَدَب   ذَهَب   دُبَ ي   دُبي

مَدينَة   إمام   لَذيذ

Exercise 3
Transliterate the words in Exercises 1 and 2 into roman script.

Exercise 4
Place the words in Exercises 1 and 2 in to the right category:

Countries	Demonstrative pronouns	Religious vocabulary	Miscellaneous

Exercise 5
What is the English equivalent of the following Arabic loanword?

باذِنْجان

Letter group no. 5: non-connectors (part II)

Rā' راء /r/   Zāy زاي /z/   Wāw واو /w/

ر	ز	و
Isolated	Isolated	Isolated

ـر	ر	ـز	ز	ـو	و
Final and Medial	Initial	Final and Medial	Initial	Final and Medial	Initial

In this unit you will learn
- *how to write and join the non-connector letters ر ز و*
- *how to read and recognize these letters in real contexts and in a variety of script styles*
- *new and commonly used vocabulary using these letters*

The fifth letter group are also non-connectors and there are three letters that all share one recognisable core shape. They are Rā' راء (ر), Zāy زاي (ز) and Wāw واو (و).

This is an easy group of letters to learn to write as all of them remain the same in all positions and never connect to any following letters (see table). The only minor difference you will notice is a single dot: Zāy (ز) has one dot above while Rā' (ر) has none.

Pay close attention to the shape of this group and do not confuse it with the previous group (د ذ). The core shape of this group has a wide angle and is written below the line.

The skeleton shape is similar to a small hook angled slightly towards the left (below 90°).

Letter group no. 5 in a nutshell

Pronunciation	Joined up	Final	Medial	Initial	Isolated	Name
/r / in roll	ر ر ر	ـر	ـر	ر	ر	راء Rā'
/z/ in zoo	ز ز ز	ـز	ـز	ز	ز	زاي Zāy
/w/ in wow	و و و	ـو	ـو	و	و	واو Wāw

Skeleton shape

Medial and Final   Isolated and Initial

HOW TO WRITE IT

In the following activity, you will learn how to write the core shape of the letters ر ز in the four different positions. Then you will practise writing all these positions connected in one imaginary word.

Following the diagram, start with the main shape, and then – in the case of the letter ز – add the dot above the letter.

Practise tracing the following and copy.

....

←

——————————————————————————————— ر ر ر   ر

——————————————————————————————— ﺮ ﺮ ﺮ   ﺮ

————————————— ر ر ر ر ر ر ر ر ر ر ر ر   ر ر ر

....

Now, repeat the same writing exercise for the letter ز. Take care to note where the dot is positioned in the letter.

IN DIFFERENT CALLIGRAPHIC STYLES

This is how ر is written in different script and calligraphy styles. The letter ز will look exactly the same, with the exception of a dot above it.

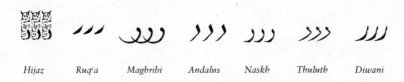

| Hijaz | Ruqʻa | Maghribi | Andalus | Naskh | Thuluth | Diwani |

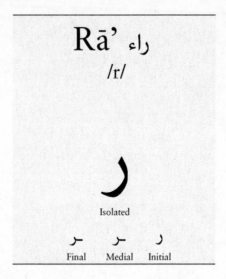

Rā' راء
/r/

ر

Isolated

ـر   ـر   ر
Final Medial Initial

The first letter of this group is Rā' راء (ر), which is the twentieth letter in the Arabic alphabet.

ر is a non-connector letter with only two different shapes (ر ـر – see table).

Pronunciation	Joined up	Final	Medial	Initial	Isolated	Name
/r/ in roll	ر ر ر	ـر	ـر	ر	ر	راء Rā'

HOW TO READ IT

The letter Rā' راء (ر) is transliterated and pronounced as frontal /r/ in the word *roll*. Notice how ر is sounded in combination with the different vowels and pronunciation symbols in the table.

Read the following letter/vowel combinations.

Supplementary vowels		Double vowels		Long vowels		Short vowels	
/rr/	رّ	/ran/	رًا	/rā/	را	/ra/	رَ
vowelless /r/	رْ	/run/	رٌ	/rū/	رو	/ru/	رُ
/rā/	رى	/rin/	رٍ	/rī/	ري	/ri/	رِ

READ AND WRITE IT IN REAL CONTEXTS

Look at how ر is combined with other letters from the previous letter groups.

Find out what letters these words are composed of, join the combinations of letters as shown here, then compare how the script is written in print and handwritten form.

Start with the main shape, then add the dots followed by the vowels.

Translation	Pronunciation	Handwriting practice	Combinations	Print form

←
Reading direction
Practise tracing the following and copy.

With long vowels

-	rā	_____ را	ر ا	را
-	rū	_____ رو	ر و	رو
-	rī	_____ ري	ر ي	ري

house	dār	_____ دار	د ا ر	دار
cold (n.)	bard	_____ برد	ب ر د	بَرْد
cold (adj.)	bārid	_____ بارد	ب ا ر د	بارِد
male	dhakar	_____ ذَكَر	ذَ كَ ر	ذَكَر
sweetcorn	dhurah	_____ ذُرَة	ذُ رَ ة	ذُرَة
dates	tamr	_____ تَمْر	تَ مْ ر	تَمَر
traffic	murūr	_____ مُرور	مُ ر و ر	مُرور
post	barīd	_____ بَريد	بَ ر ي د	بَريد

tickets	tadhākir	_____ تَذاكِر	ت ذ ا كِ ر	تَذاكِر
Iran	īrān	_____ إيران	إ ي ر ا ن	إيران
Jordan	al-'urdun	_____ الأُرْدُن	ا ل أ رْ دُ ن	الأُرْدُن
Emirates	al-'imārāt	_____ الإمارات	ا ل إ م ا ر ا ت	الإمارات
Desire (name)	murād[1]	_____ مُراد	مُ ر ا د	مُراد
Mary	mariam	_____ مَرْيَم	مَ رْ يَ م	مَرْيَم

---

[1] This is the author's first name.

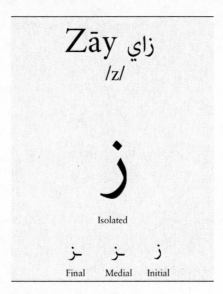

Zāy زاي
/z/

ز

Isolated

ـز   ـزـ   ز

Final   Medial   Initial

The first letter of this group is Zāy زاي (ز), which is the twenty-first letter in the Arabic alphabet.

ز is a non-connector letter with only two different shapes (ز ـز – see table).

Pronunciation	Joined up	Final	Medial	Initial	Isolated	Name
/z/ in zoo	ز ز ز	ـز	ـزـ	ز	ز	زاي Zāy

HOW TO READ IT

The letter Zāy (ز) is transliterated and pronounced as /z/ in zoo.

Notice how ز is sounded in combination with the different vowels and pronunciation symbols in the table.

Read the following letter/vowel combinations.

Supplementary vowels		Double vowels		Long vowels		Short vowels	
/zz/	زّ	/zan/	زًا	/zā/	زا	/za/	زَ
vowelless /z/	زْ	/zun/	زٌ	/zū/	زو	/zu/	زُ
/zā/	زى	/zin/	زٍ	/zī/	زي	/zi/	زِ

READ AND WRITE IT IN REAL CONTEXTS

Look at how the letter ز is combined with other letters from the previous letter groups.

Find out what letters these words are composed of, join the combinations of letters as shown here, then compare how the script is written in print and handwritten form.

Start with the main shape, then add the dots followed by the vowels.

Translation	Pronunciation	Handwriting practice	Combinations	Print form

←
Reading direction
Practise tracing the following and copy.

With long vowels

-	zā	_____ زا	ز ا	زا
-	zū	_____ زو	ز و	زو
-	zī	_____ زي	ز ي	زي

88

rice	'arozz	أُرُزّ	أُ رُ زّ	أُرُزّ
raisins	zabīb	زَبِيب	زَ ب ي ب	زَبيب
butter	zubdah	زُبْدَة	زُ بْ دَ ة	زُبْدَة
oil	zayt	زَيْت	زَ يْ ت	زَيْت
olive	zaytūn	زَيْتون	زَ يْ ت و ن	زَيْتون
olive oil	zayt a(l)z-zaytūn	زَيْت الزَّيْتون	زَ يْ ت ال زَّ يْ ت و ن	زَيْت الزَّيْتون
to visit	zāra	زارَ	زا رَ	زارَ
bazaar	bazār	بَزار	بَ ز ا ر	بَزار
earthquake	zilzāl	زِلْزال	زِ لْ ز ا ل	زِلْزال
residence	nazal	نَزَل	نَ زَ ل	نَزَل
house	manzil	مَنْزِل	مَ نْ زِ ل	مَنْزِل
name of a famous well in Mecca, Saudi Arabia	zamzam	زَمْزَم	زَ مْ زَ م	زَمْزَم
prison cell	zinzānah	زِنْزانة	زِ نْ ز ا ن ة	زِنْزانة
Hotel Holland	nazal hūlandā	نَزَل هولانْدا	نَ زَ ل ه و ل ا نْ د ا	نَزَل هولاندا

ماكدونالدز_____

Do you recognize the name of this famous fast-food chain?

What is the subtitle written on this cola can?

The letter Wāw حَرْفُ الواو

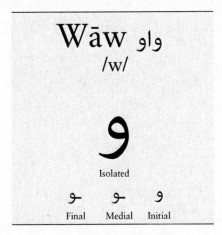

Wāw واو
/w/

و

Isolated

ـو   ـو   و

Final   Medial   Initial

The third letter of this group is the letter Wāw واو (و), which is the twenty-seventh letter in the Arabic alphabet.

و is a non-connector letter with only two different shapes (و – ـو see table).

The letter و shares the basic shape of the fifth letter group but with an oval loop.

Pronunciation	Joined up	Final	Medial	Initial	Isolated	Name
/w/ in wow	و و و	ـو	ـو	و	و واو	Wāw

HOW TO WRITE IT

Skeleton shape

Medial and Final   Isolated and Initial

In the following activity, you will learn how to write the core shape of the letter و in the four different positions.

Then you will practise writing all these positions connected in one imaginary word.

Following the diagram of the skeleton shape, practise tracing the following and copy.

←

و

و و و   و

ـو ـو ـو   ـو

و و و و و و و و و و و و   و و و

IN DIFFERENT CALLIGRAPHIC STYLES

Hijaz	*Ruqʿa*	*Maghribi*	*Andalus*	*Naskh*	*Thuluth*	*Diwani*

READ AND WRITE IT IN REAL CONTEXTS

Look at how و is combined with other letters from the previous letter groups.

Find out what letters these words are composed of, join the combinations of letters as shown, then compare how the script is written in print and handwritten form.

Start with the main shape, then add the dots followed by the vowels.

Translation	Pronunciation	Handwriting practice	Combinations	Print form

←
Reading direction
Practise tracing the following and copy.

With long vowels

-	wā	وا	و ا	وا
-	wū	وو	و و	وو
-	wī	وي	و ي	وي

fabrics	thawb	ثَوْب	ثَ وْ ب	ثَوْب
rose	wardah	وَرْدَة	وَ رْ دَ ة	وَرْدَة
roses	wurūd	وُرود	وُ ر و د	وُرود
or	'aw	أَوْ	أَ وْ	أَوْ
air	hawā'	هَواء	هَ و ا ء	هَواء
agency	wakālah	وَكالَة	وَ ك ا لَ ة	وَكالة
Kuwait	dawlat al-kuwait	دَوْلَة الكُوَيْت	دَ وْ لَ ة ال كُ وَ يْ ت	دَوْلة الكُوَيْت
water and air	mā'wa hawā'	ماء وَهَواء	مَ ا ء وَ هَ و ا ء	ماء وَهَواء

QUICK VOCAB

Coat of arms of Kuwait

Days of the week

So far you have learned the days Monday (الاِثْنَين) and Tuesday (الثُّلاثاء). This is how to say and write the word "day" in Arabic.

day	yawm	_____	يَوْم	يَ وْ م	يَوْم
days	'ayyām	_____	أيّام	أ يّ ا م	أيّام

Hamza on Wāw (ؤ)

As we mentioned in Unit 1, the Hamza sign (ء) can be carried by three different consonantal seats, one of which is the letter Wāw واو (و).

Read and copy the following examples.

teacher	mu'addib	_____	مُؤَدِّب	مُ ؤَ دِّ ب	مُؤَدِّب
caller of prayer	mu'adhdhin	_____	مُؤَذِّن	مُ ؤَ ذِّ ن	مُؤَذِّن
pearls	lu'lu'	_____	لُؤْلُؤ	لُ ؤْ لُ ؤ	لُؤْلُؤ

Hamza on the Yā' (ئ)

Finally, the third carrier of the Hamza sign (ء) is the letter Yā' ياء (ي).

Read and copy the following examples.

always	dā'iman	_____	دائماً	د ا ئ م أ	دَائِماً
smell	rā'ihah	رائِحة	_____	ر ا ئ ح ة	رائِحَة
innocent	barī'	_____	بَريئ	بَ ر ي ئ	بَريئ

Insight

Here are some more Arabic loanwards you already know.

admiral	'amīr al-	_____	أميرال-	أ م ي ر ال-	أَميرال
hazard	a(l)z-zahr	_____	الزَّهر	ا ل زَّ هـْ ر	الزَّهر
vizier	waz īr	_____	وَزير	و ز ي ر	وَزير
valley	wādī	_____	وادي	و ا د ي	وادي
bazār	bazār	_____	بَزار	بَ ز ا ر	بَزار

ARABIC QUOTATION حِكْمَة عَرَبِيَّة

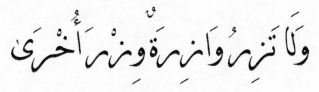

walā taziru wāziratun wizra ukhrā

That no burdened person (with sins) shall bear the burden
(sins) of another

Qur'an (Chapter 35, Verse 18)

Circle the letters ر ز و wherever you see them in the quotation.

The following table is a summary of what you need to know about the letters و ر ز.

Pronun- ciation	Joined up	Final	Medial	Initial	Isolated	Name
/r/ in roll	ر ر ر	ـر	ـر	ر	ر	راء Rāʾ
/z/ in zoo	ز ز ز	ـز	ـز	ز	ز	زاي Zāy
/w/ in wow	و و و	ـو	ـو	و	و	واو Wāw

Test yourself

Exercise 1
Read out loud and combine the letters to form words.

ت ذ ا ك ر   وَرْدَة   ال إ م ا ر ا ت الإمارات

مَ نْ زِ ل   هَ و ا ء   دَوْلَة

Exercise 2
Read out loud and write the unjoined forms of the letters that make up the following words.

بَريد   يَوْم   ب ا رِ د   بارِد

زَيْتون   الأُرْدُن   أَرُز

Exercise 3
Transliterate the words in Exercises 1 and 2 into roman script.

Exercise 4
Place the words in Exercises 1 and 2 into the right category.

Food	Countries	Public signs	Adjectives	Miscellaneous

Exercise 5
How do we say the following Arabic loanwords in English?

أَميرال- الزَّهـْر   بَزار   وَزير

Exercise 6
Read the following and translate into English.

زَيْت الزَّيْتون

Unit **6**

Letter group no. 6

Jīm جيم /j/

Ḥā' حاء /ḥ/

Khā' خاء /kh/

ج
Isolated

ح
Isolated

خ
Isolated

ج	جـ	جـ	ح	حـ	حـ	خ	خـ	خـ
Final	Medial	Initial	Final	Medial	Initial	Final	Medial	Initial

In this unit you will learn
- *how to write and join the letters ج ح خ*
- *how to read and recognize the letters in real contexts in a variety of script styles*
- *new and commonly used words*

The sixth letter group has three letters which all share one recognizable core shape. They are Jīm جيمٌ (ج), Ḥā' خاء (خ) and Khā' خاء (خ) in alphabetical order.

98

This is an easy group of letters to learn to write as all of them are exactly identical in all positions (see table). The only minor difference you will notice is the number and position of a single dot: Jīm ج has one dot below, Ḥā' ح has no dots while Khā' خ has one above.

All three letters are connecting consonants with four different shapes.

Letter group no. 6 in a nutshell

Pronunciation	Joined up	Final	Medial	Initial	Isolated	Name
/j/ in jam, game or visual	ججج	ج	ـجـ	جـ	ج	جيم Jīm
/h/ in hot	ححح	ح	ـحـ	حـ	ح	حاء Ḥā'
/kh/ in Scottish loch	خخخ	خ	ـخـ	خـ	خ	خاء Khā'

HOW TO WRITE IT

Skeleton shape

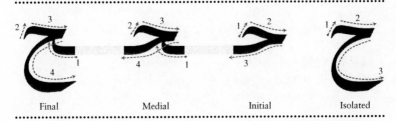

Final   Medial   Initial   Isolated

In the following activity, you will learn how to write the core shape of the letters خ ح ج in the four positions. Then you will practise writing all these positions connected in one imaginary word.

Bear in mind:

1 The initial and medial forms are written above the line
(ﺟ ﺣ ﺧ).
2 In the isolated and final form, the tail dips below the line with
a distinct tail similar to half-closed circle (ﺦ ﺢ ﺞ).

*Following the diagram of the selection shape, practise tracing the
following and copy.*

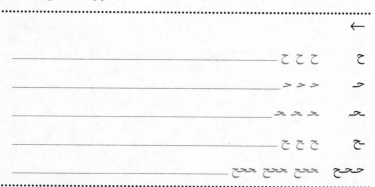

Now, repeat the same writing exercise for the letters ﺥ ﺡ as in the
example. Notice where the dot is positioned in each letter: above
the core shape in ﺥ and below it in ﺡ.

IN DIFFERENT CALLIGRAPHIC STYLES

This is how Ḥā' ﺡ is written in different script and calligraphy
styles. The letters Jīm ﺝ and Khā' ﺥ will look exactly the same,
with the exception of a dot below ﺝ and one above ﺥ.

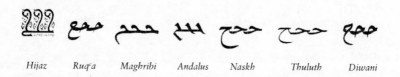

Hijaz   Ruq'a   Maghribi   Andalus   Naskh   Thuluth   Diwani

The letter Jīm حَرْفُ الجيم

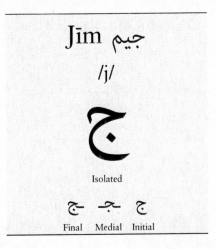

Jīm جيم

/j/

ج

Isolated

جـ ـجـ ـج
Final Medial Initial

The first letter of this group is Jīm جيم (ج), which is the fifth letter in the Arabic alphabet.

ج is a connector letter with four different shapes (ج جـ ـجـ ـج – see table).

Pronunciation	Joined up	Final	Medial	Initial	Isolated	Name
/j/ in jam	ججج	ـج	ـجـ	جـ	ج	جيم Jīm

HOW TO READ IT

Depending on the dialect spoken, the letter Jīm (ج) can be transliterated and pronounced in three different ways:

1 As /j/ in *judge* or *George* in classical Arabic.
2 As /g/ in *game* or *gallery* famously in Lower Egypt, Gulf region and other parts of the Arab world.
3 As in the French /j/ in *jour* or as in the English word *visual*, mostly in north African Arab countries (Morocco, Algeria and Tunisia).

Notice how ج is sounded in combination with the different vowels and pronunciation symbols in the table.

Read the following letter/vowel combinations.

Try reading the letter ج in the three different ways, as explained earlier.

Supplementary vowels		Double vowels		Long vowels		Short vowels	
/jj/	جّ	/jan/	جاً	/jā/	جا	/ja/	جَ
vowelless /j/	جْ	/jun/	جٌ	/jū/	جو	/ju/	جُ
/jā/	جى	/jin/	جٍ	/jī/	جي	/ji/	جِ

READ AND WRITE IT IN REAL CONTEXTS

Look at how ج is combined with other letters from the previous letter groups. Find out what letters these words are composed of, then join the combinations of letters as shown.

Start with the main shape, then add the dots followed by the vowels.

Translation	Pronunciation	Handwriting practice	Combinations	Print form

←
Reading direction
Practise tracing the following and copy.

With long vowels

-	jā	_____ جا	ج ا	جا
-	jū	_____ جو	ج و	جو
-	jī	_____ جي	ج ي	جي

Family

Here are other important family members spelled with ج you should learn.

grandfather	jadd	جَدّ	جَ دّ	جَدّ
grandmother	jaddah[1]	جَدَّة	جَ دّ ة	جَدَّة
husband	zawj	زَوْج	زَ وْ ج	زَوْج
wife	zawjah	زَوْجَة	زَ وْ جَ ة	زَوْجَة

Notice that the only difference between the masculine and feminine of grandfather جَدّ and husband زَوْج is simply the feminine ending ة/ـة.

chicken	dajāj	دَجاج	دَ ج ا ج	دَجاج
carrot	jazar	جَزَر	جَ زَ ر	جَزَر
butcher	jazzār	جَزَّار	جَ زّ ا ر	جَزَّار
men's toilets	dawrat miyaah li(l)-rrijāl	دَوْرَة مِياه للرِّجال	دَ وْ رَ ة م ي ا ه ل ل رِ ج ا ل	دَوْرَة مِياه للرِّجال

---

[1] Do not confuse this word with the name of the Saudi Arabian city Jeddah جِدَّة!

Algeria	al-jazā'ir	_____	الجَزائِر الجَزائِر ال جَ ز ا ئِ ر
Aljazeera	al-jazeerah	_____	الجَزيرَة الجَزيرَة ال جَ ز ي رَ ة

al-jazeera

As you already know, Al-Jazeera الجَزيرَة is the name of an international news channel based in Qatar. The literal meaning of الجَزيرَة is "The Island", in reference to the Arabian peninsula الجَزيرَة العربية.

The letter Hā' حَرْفُ الحاء

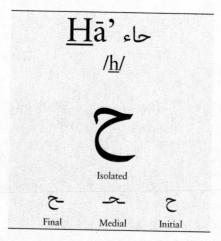

Hā' حاء

/h/

ح
Isolated

ح   ح   ح
Final   Medial   Initial

The second letter of this group in alphabetical order is letter Hā' (ح) ح ء, which is the sixth letter in the Arabic alphabet.

ح is a connector letter with four different shapes (ح حح حح – see table).

Pronunciation	Joined up	Final	Medial	Initial	Isolated	Name
<u>h</u> in hot	حح حح	ح	ـحـ	حـ	ح	حاء <u>Hā'</u>

HOW TO READ IT

The sound of the letter <u>Hā'</u> (ح) has no equivalent in English. It is pronounced like a loud whispering from the throat much like when you breathe to clean your glasses.

It is transliterated as /<u>h</u>/ with a dash underneath to differentiate it from Hā' (ه) /h/. Make sure you do not confuse the sound of the Hā' ه with that of the <u>Hā'</u> ح.

Now, pay attention to how you pronounce the following similar sounding examples:

/hubuub/ blowing	هُبوب	vs.	حُبوب	/<u>h</u>ubuub/ cereals

Notice how the letter <u>Hā'</u> (ح) is sounded in combination with the different vowels and pronunciation symbols in the table.

Read the following letter/vowel combinations.

Supplementary vowels		Double vowels		Long vowels		Short vowels	
/<u>h</u>h/	حّ	/<u>h</u>an/	حًا	/<u>h</u>ā/	حا	/<u>h</u>a/	حَ
vowelless /<u>h</u>/	حْ	/<u>h</u>un/	حٌ	/<u>h</u>ū/	حو	/<u>h</u>u/	حُ
/<u>h</u>ā/	حى	/<u>h</u>in/	حٍ	/<u>h</u>ī/	حي	/<u>h</u>i/	حِ

READ AND WRITE IT IN REAL CONTEXTS

Look at how ح is combined with other letters from the previous letter groups.

Find out what letters these words are composed of, then join the combinations of letters as shown.

Translation	Pronunciation	Handwriting practice	Combinations	Print form

← Reading direction
Practise tracing the following and copy.

With long vowels

-	ḥā	حا	ح ا	حا
-	ḥū	حو	ح و	حو
-	ḥī	حي	ح ي	حي

Numbers

1	wāḥid/ah	واحِد/ة	و ا ح د/ ة	واحِد/ة
١ 1st (m.)	'awwal	أوَّل	أ وَّ ل	أوَّل
1st (f.)	'ūlā	أولى	أ و ل ى	أولى

Days of the week
Linguistically speaking, Sunday الأَحَد is regarded as the first day of the week, which is why its name is derived from واحِد wāḥid, i.e. one.

| Sunday | al-'aḥad | الأَحَد | ا ل أ ح َد | الأَحَد |

Colours

The well-known tourist attraction, Alhambra (i.e. the red one), originally named "the red fortress" (الْقَلْعَةُ ٱلْحَمْرَاء), is a famous palace built during the 14th century by the Arab/Muslim rulers in the city of Granada in Spain. If you visit Alhambra, you will be surprised to notice Arabic inscriptions written in calligraphy around the palace walls.

الْحَمْرَاء pronounced as /al-hamrā'/ means red (feminine – the masculine form is أَحْمَر /'aḥmar).

red (f.)	al-ḥamrā'	_____ الحَمْرَاء	ا ل حَ مْ ر ا ء	الحَمْرَاء
red (m.)	'aḥmar	_____ أحْمَر	أَ حْ مَ ر	أَحْمَر

QUICK VOCAB

Insight

Common Arabic names

It is universally known that the name مُحَمَّد Muhammad is one of the most common given names in the world (including variations), with an estimate of more than 15 million people worldwide carrying the name Muhammad[2]. مُحَمَّد can also be spelled as Muhammed or Mohammed. The name is derived from the root word ح م د h-m-d, i.e. to praise.

---

[2] Columbia Encyclopedia 2000.

Calligraphic writing of Muhammad in traditional Thuluth calligraphy by Hattat Aziz

Muhammad (praiseworthy)	muḥammad	_____	مُحَمَّد	مُحَمَّد مُ حَ مَّ د
Ahmad	'aḥmad	_____	أَحْمَد	أَحْمَد أَ حْ مَ د
Mahmoud	maḥmūd	_____	مَحْمود	مَحْمود مَ حْ م و د

Spoken Arabic

welcome	marḥaban	_____	مَرْحباً	مَرْحباً مَ رْ حَ ب اً
praise be to Allah	al-ḥamdu lillāh	_____	الحَمْدُ لله	الحَمْدُ لله ال حَ مْ دُ لِ لَّ ه

الحَمْدُ لله مَرْحَباً

Al-hamdu lillāh الحَمْدُ لله is a typical common reply to "How are you" among Arabs and Muslims. Notice that الحَمْدُ لله is also derived from the same root word (ح م د) h-m-d, i.e. to praise, as the name مُحَمَّد.

108

Bahrain	al-ba<u>h</u>rayn	_____	البَحْرَيْن ا ل بَ حْ رَ يْ ن البَحْرَيْن
Doha³	a(l)d-daw<u>h</u>a	_____	الدَّوْحَة ا ل دَّ وْ حَ ة الدَّوْحَة
love	<u>h</u>ub	_____	حُبَّ حُ بَّ حُبَّ
lover	<u>h</u>abīb	_____	حَبيب/ة حَ ب ي ب /ة حَبيب/ة

كُلّ ما أُحِبّ

كُ لَّ م ا ا أُ حِ بّ

كُلَ ما أُحِبّ _____

kull mā 'uhibb

Lit. everything I love

Food and drink

حَلَوِيات

حَ لَ وِ ي ا ت

حَلَوِيات _____

<u>h</u>alaweyāt

pastry (shop)

What is the name of this pastry shop?

(Hint: the letter س / ـس is pronounced as /s/ in *seen*.)

حَلَوِيات is the plural of حَلْوى, i.e. sweets or sweet pastry. To describe the sweetness of any food item, we say حُلْوْ, i.e. sweet. Now practise writing these words.

---

² Capital of قطر Qatar.

---

candy	halwā	_____	حَلْوى	حَ لْ و ى	حَلْوى
sweet	hulw	_____	حُلْوْ	حُ لْ وْ	حُلْوْ
milk	halīb	_____	حَليب	حَ ل ي ب	حَليب
salt	milh	_____	مِلْح	م ِلْ ح	مِلْح
soup	harīrah	_____	حَريرة	حَ ر ي ر ة	حَريرة

حَريرة is a famous tomato and lentil soup in Morocco and is considered to be one of Morocco's national dishes. Although it is consumed throughout the year, it has always been favoured as the best dish to break the fast with at sunset during the holy month of Ramadan.

bathroom	hammām	_____	حَمّام	حَ مّ ا م	حَمّام
around	hawla	_____	حَوْلَ	حَ وْ لَ	حَوْلَ
under, beneath	tahta	_____	تَحْتَ	تَ حْ تَ	تَحْتَ
we	nahnu	_____	نَحْنُ	نَ حْ نُ	نَحْنُ

110

The letter Khā' حَرْفُ الحاء

Khā' خاء
/kh/

خ
Isolated

خ ـخ خ ـخ
Final Medial Initial

The third letter of this group is letter Khā' خاء (خ), which is the seventh letter in the Arabic alphabet.

خ is a connector letter with four different shapes (خ خخخ).

Pronunciation	Joined up	Final	Medial	Initial	Isolated	Name
/kh/ in Scottish "lo<u>ch</u>"	خخخ	ـخ	ـخـ	خـ	خ	خاء Khā'

HOW TO READ IT

The letter Khā' (خ) is a sound common in many languages. It is transliterated as /kh/ and pronounced like the Scottish *loch* or the Spanish *juntos*.

Notice how خ is sounded in combination with the different vowels and pronunciation symbols in the table.

Read the following letter/vowel combinations.

Supplementary vowels		Double vowels		Long vowels		Short vowels	
/khkh/	خْخَ	/khan/	خاً	/khā/	خا	/kha/	خَ
vowelless /kh/	خْ	/khun/	خٌ	/khū/	خو	/khu/	خُ
/khā/	خى	/khin/	خٍ	/khī/	خي	/khi/	خِ

READ AND WRITE IT IN REAL CONTEXTS

Look at how خ is combined with other letters from the previous letter groups.

Find out what letters these words are composed of, then join the combinations of letters as shown.

Start with the main shape, then add the dots followed by the vowels.

Translation	Pronunciation	Handwriting practice	Combinations	Print form

←
Reading direction
Practise tracing the following and copy.

With long vowels

-	khā	خا	خ ا	خا
-	khū	خو	خ و	خو
-	khī	خي	خ ي	خي

Family members

Here are some members of the family in Arabic that are spelled with خ.

English	Transliteration			
brother	'akh	أخ _____	أ خ	أَخ
sister	'ukht	أُخت _____	أ خ ت	أُخْت
maternal uncle	khāl	خال _____	خ ا ل	خال
maternal aunt	khālah	خالَة _____	خ ا لَ ة	خالة

bread	khubz	خُبْز _____	خُ بْ ز	خُبز
peach	khawkh	خَوْخ _____	خَ وْ خ	خَوْخ
entry	dukhūl	دُخول _____	دُ خ و ل	دُخول

exit	khurūj	خُروج _____	خُ ر و ج	خُروج

new	jadīd	جَديد _____	جَ د ي د	جَديد
allowed (according to Islamic law)	<u>h</u>alāl	حَلال _____	حَ لَ ا ل	حَلال

QUICK VOCAB

You already speak Arabic!

Camel *jamal* جَمَل is a loanword.

Sugar is derived from Arabic *sukkar* and originally from Persian *shaker*, that is "ground or candied sugar".

Magazine *makhazin* is taken from the Arabic مَخَازِن, plural of مَخْزَن *makhzan*, i.e. "storehouse". Originally, it meant "a printed list of military stores and information".

Alcohol comes from the Arabic الكُحْل *al-kuhl*, i.e. "the fine metallic powder used to darken the eyelids". This definition was later extended to "any sublimated substance, the pure spirit of anything".

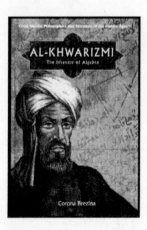

Algebra *al-jabr* الجَبر in Arabic means "reunion of broken parts" initially used by al-Khwarizmi as the title of his famous treatise on equations "Kitab al-Jabr w'al-Muqabala", *Rules of Reintegration and Reduction*.

Algorithm *al-khawārizmī* الخوارزمي is the surname of a well-known Muslim mathematician in Baghdad, Abu Ja'far Muhammad ibn Musa al-Khwarismi who pioneered sophisticated mathematics, including algebra. Algorithm (an anglicized form of *al-khawārizmī*) is currently used for calculation, computer science and many other related fields.

ARABIC QUOTATION حِكْمَة عَرَبِيَّة

$$\text{مَنْ جَدَّ وَجَدَ ومَنْ زَرَعَ حصَدَ}$$

man jadda wajada wa man zara‘a <u>h</u>a<u>s</u>a<u>d</u>a
He who perseveres finds and he who sows harvests

Arabic proverb

Circle the letters ج ح wherever you see them in the quotation. Do you recognize any familiar words in the quotation that you have learned so far?

SUMMARY TABLE

The following table is a summary of what you need to know about the letters ح ج خ.

Pronunciation	Joined up	Final	Medial	Initial	Isolated	Name
/j/ in jam, game or visual	ججج	ـج	ـجـ	جـ	ج	Jīm جيم
/h/ in hat	ححح	ـح	ـحـ	حـ	ح	Hā’ حاء
/kh/ in Scottish loch	خخخ	ـخ	ـخـ	خـ	خ	Khā’ خاء

Test yourself

Exercise 1
Read out loud and combine the letters to form words.

خُبْز   خُ بْ ز   مِ لْ ح   حَ ل ي ب

دَ ج ا ج   مُ حَ مَّ د   ا ل أَ حَ د

Exercise 2
Read out loud and write the unjoined forms of the letters that
make up the following words.

جَدَّة   جَ دّ ة   واحِد   أَحْمَر

البَحْرَيْن   الجَزائِر   أخ

Exercise 3
Transliterate the words in Exercises 1 and 2 into roman script.

Exercise 4
Place the words in Exercises 1 and 2 into the right category.

Food	Countries	Colours	Family	Numbers	Arabic names

Exercise 5
What is the English equivalent of the following Arabic loanwords?

الجَبْر   جَمَل   الكُحول   مَخازِن

Exercise 6
Read the following expression and translate into English.

مَرْحباً

Exercise 7
Convert the following into the feminine.

جَدّ خال حَبيب زَوْج

Unit **7**

الوِحْدَة السابِعَة

....

Letter group no. 7

Shīn شين
/sh/

Sīn سين
/s/

ش
Isolated

ش ـشـ شـ
Final   Medial   Initial

س
Isolated

ـس ـسـ سـ
Final   Medial   Initial

In this unit you will learn
- *how to write and join the letters ش س*
- *how to read and recognize the letters in real contexts in a variety of script styles*
- *new and commonly used words*

Now we come to the seventh letter group. This is another group that has only two letters that share one recognizable core letter shape (س). They are Sīn سين (س) and Shīn شين (ش), in alphabetical order.

This is an easy letter group to write and pronounce as the sounds /s/ and /sh/ are familiar to the English ear. In writing the script, the only apparent difference you will notice between the two letters is that Shīn ش has three dots above, while Sīn س has no dots at all.

The two letters are connecting consonants with four slightly different shapes.

The skeleton basic shape has the following features:

1 The core shape is distinctly recognisable by three little hooks or teeth.
2 The tail of the letter is similar to the letter Nūn ن.
3 In handwriting, these hooks are usually written as a straight line.

Letter group no. 7 in a nutshell

Pronun-ciation	Joined up	Final	Medial	Initial	Isolated	Name
/s/ in seen	سسس	ـس	ـسـ	سـ	س	سين Sīn
/sh/ in sheep	ششش	ـش	ـشـ	شـ	ش	شين Shīn

HOW TO WRITE IT

Skeleton shape

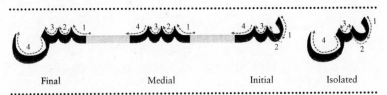

| Final | Medial | Initial | Isolated |

In the following activity, you will learn how to write the core skeleton shape of the letters س ش in the four different positions. Then you will practise writing all these positions connected in one imaginary word.

Following the diagram of the skeleton shape, practise tracing the following and copy.

←

_____	س س س	س
_____	س س س	س
_____	ـس ـس ـس	ـس
_____	ـسـ ـسـ ـسـ	ـسـ
_____	سـ سـ سـ	سـ
_____	سسس سسس سسس	سـسـس

Now, repeat the same writing exercise for the letter ش. Notice where the three dots are positioned in the letter.

IN DIFFERENT CALLIGRAPHIC STYLES

This is how Sīn س is written in different script and calligraphy styles. The letter Shīn ش will look exactly the same, with the exception of the three dots above.

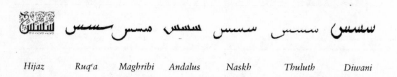

Hijaz	*Ruqʻa*	*Maghribi*	*Andalus*	*Naskh*	*Thuluth*	*Diwani*

The letter Sīn حَرْفُ السِّين

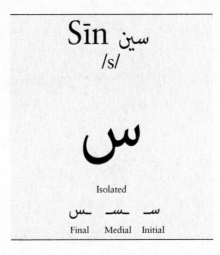

سين Sīn
/s/

س

Isolated

سـ ـسـ ـس
Final Medial Initial

The first letter of this group is letter Sīn سين (س), which is the twelfth letter in the Arabic alphabet.

س is a connector letter with four different shapes (س سسس) (see table).

Pronun-ciation	Joined up	Final	Medial	Initial	Isolated	Name
/s/ in seen	سسس	ـس	ـسـ	سـ	س	سين Sīn

HOW TO READ IT

س is transliterated and pronounced as /s/ as in the word *scene* and *Sam*.

Do not confuse the two sounds Sīn س and Thā' ث. Pay attention to how you pronounce the following similar sounding examples:

/hāris/ guardian, keeper	حارِس	vs	حارِث	/hārith/ ploughman

Notice how س is sounded in combination with the different vowels and pronunciation symsbols in the table.

Read the following letter/vowel combinations.

Supplementary vowels		Double vowels		Long vowels		Short vowels	
/ss/	سّ	/san/	سًا	/sā/	سا	/sa/	سَ
vowelless /s/	سْ	/sun/	سٌّ	/sū/	سو	/su/	سُ
/sā/	سى	/sin/	سٍّ	/sī/	سي	/si/	سِ

READ AND WRITE IT IN REAL CONTEXTS

Look at how س is combined with other letters from the previous letter groups.

Find out what letters these words are composed of, join the combinations of letters as shown, and compare how the script is written in print and handwritten form.

Start with the main shape, then add the dots followed by the vowels.

Translation	Pronunciation	Handwriting practice	Combinations	Print form

$\leftarrow$
Reading direction
Practise tracing the following and copy.

With long vowels

-	sā	ــــــــــ سا	س ا	سا
-	sū	ــــــــــ سو	س و	سو
-	sī	ــــــــــ سي	س ي	سي

Numbers

٥	5	khamsah	_____ خَمْسَة	خَ مْ سَ ة	خَمْسَة
	5th	khāmis	_____ خامِس	خ ا مِ س	خامِس
	50	khamsūn	_____ خَمْسون	خَ مْ س و ن	خَمْسون
	1/5	khumus	_____ خُمُس	خُ مُ س	خُمُس
٦	6	sittah	_____ سِتَّة	سِ تَّ ة	سِتَّة
	6th	sādis	_____ سادِس	س ا دِ س	سادِس
	60	sittūn	_____ سِتّون	سِ تّ و ن	سِتّون
	1/6	sudus	_____ سُدُس	سُ دُ س	سُدُس

Days of the week

So far you have learned how to read and write Monday, Tuesday
and Sunday. What about Thursday and Saturday?

Thursday	al-khamīs	_____ الخَميس	ال خَ م ي س	الخَميس
Saturday	a(l)s-sābt	_____ السّبْت	ال سّ بْ ت	السّبْت

Syria	sūriyā	_____ سوريا	س و رْ يا	سوريا
Sudan	a(l)s-sūdān	_____ السّودان	ال سّ و د ا ن	السّودان
Tunisia	tūnis	_____ تونِس	ت و نِ س	تونِس
couscous	kuskus	_____ كُسكُس	كُ سْ كُ س	كُسكُس
fish	samak	_____ سَمَك	سَ مَ ك	سَمَك

Commonly used Islamic terms

Among frequently used words in Arabic, especially among Muslims (Arabs and non-Arabs alike), are words and expressions derived from the root word s-l-m سلم, i.e. to be safe and sound, e.g. Islam, Muslim, etc. Here are some examples.

peace, safety	salām		سلام	سَ ل ا م	سَلام
security, safety	salāmah		سلامة	سَ ل ا مَ ة	سَلامة
Islam	'islām		إسلام	إ سْ ل ا م	إسْلام
Muslim m./f.	muslim /ah		مُسلِم /ة	مُ سْ لِ م/ة	مُسْلِم/ة
safe, sound m./f.	salīm /ah		سَلِيم/ة	سَ ل ي م/ة	سَليم/ة

Insight

a(l)s-salāmu ʿalaikum السَّلام عَلَيْكُم is one of the most common greetings in spoken Arabic, especially among Muslims (Arabs and non-Arabs). It is not time restricted and so can be used at any time of the day. The expression is mostly said in the plural and may be used even with one person, either in the masculine or the feminine.

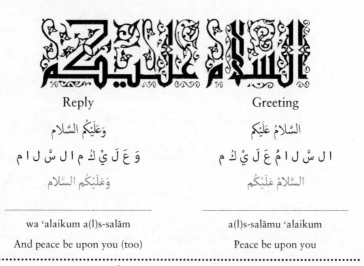

Reply	Greeting
وَعَلَيْكُم السَّلام	السَّلامُ عَلَيْكُم
وَ عَ لَ يْ كُ م ا ل سَّ ل ا م	ا ل سَّ ل ا مُ عَ لَ يْ كُ م
وَعَلَيْكُم السَّلام	السَّلامُ عَلَيْكُم

| wa ʿalaikum a(l)s-salām | a(l)s-salāmu ʿalaikum |
| And peace be upon you (too) | Peace be upon you |

QUICK VOCAB

black m.	'aswad	_____	أسْوَد	أ سْ وَ د	أسْوَد
black f.	sawdā'	_____	سَوْداء	سَ وْ د ا ء	سَوْداء
pull	'is-hab	_____	إسْحَبْ	ا ِسْ حَ بْ	إسْحَبْ

PULL

Forms of address

Mr	sayyid	_____ سيِّد	سَ يِّ د	سَيِّد
Mrs	sayyidah	_____ سَيِّدَة	سَ يِّ دَ ة	سَيِّدَة
Miss	'ānisah	_____ آنِسة	آ نِ سَ ة	آنِسَة
Dr	duktūrah	دُكْتور/ة _____ دُكْتور/ة	دُ كْ ت و ر/ة	دُكْتور/ة

Mr (سَيِّد) is used in formal communication, either spoken or written.
Mrs (سَيِّدَة) is used in formal communication with married women.
Miss (آنِسَة) is used with unmarried women.
Dr (دُكْتور/ة) is used to address professionals from the medical field
or other academic disciplines.

Circle the letters you have learned so far. How many times do they
occur in this sign?

Can you work out what this foreign sign says?

_____

Western Union

Practise writing the word here.

ويِسْتِرْن يونْيون

وِ ي سْ تِ رْ ن ي و نْ ي و ن

ويِسْتِرْن يونْيون_____

The Harry Potter films are popular globally, and the Arab world is no exception. The word "cinema", which is a borrowed word in Arabic, remains intact and is pronounced exactly the same.

Practise writing the word here.

سينما

س ي ن م ا

سينما_____

Cinema

The name of this cinema is a(l)r-rif الريف, i.e. countryside. The letter ف at the end of the second word is pronounced as /f/ in *five* (see Unit 10).

This is the sign of a cultural and foreign language institution in Morocco.

Circle the letters you have learned so far. How many times do they occur in this sign? Can you work out the meaning of the first and third word?

You might have difficulty reading the script in this sign as it is not vowelled.

Read aloud and practise writing the vowelled script.

دُروس اللُّغَة الإسْبانِيَّة

durūs a(l)l-lugha al-'isbāniyyah

Spanish language lessons

التَّسْجِيلات مَفْتوحَة

a(l)t-tasjīlāt maftūha

Registrations are open

دُروس اللُّغَة الإسْبانِيَّة _____

التَّسْجِيلات مَفْتوحَة _____

(Hints: The letter ـف in the fifth word is pronounced as /f/ in *five*. The letter ـغـ is pronounced as /gh/ in French *Paris*.)

The Letter Shīn حَرْفُ الشّين

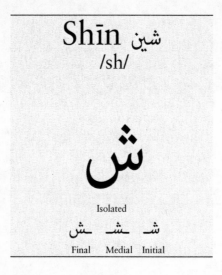

Shīn شين
/sh/

ش

Isolated

ـش ـشـ شـ
Final Medial Initial

The second letter in this group is Shīn شين (ش), which is the thirteenth letter in the Arabic alphabet.

ش is a connector letter with four different shapes (ش ششش – see table).

Pronun-ciation	Joined up	Final	Medial	Initial	Isolated	Name
/sh/ in sheep	ششش	ـش	ـشـ	شـ	ش	شين Shīn

HOW TO READ IT

ش is transliterated and pronounced as /sh/ as in the word _sheep_ and _shoe_.

Notice how ش is sounded in combination with the different vowels and pronunciation symsbols in the table.

Read the following letter/vowel combinations.

Supplementary Vowels		Double vowels		Long vowels		Short vowels	
/shsh/	شّ	/shan/	شاً	/shā/	شا	/sha/	شَ
Vowelless /sh/	شْ	/shun/	شٌ	/shū/	شو	/shu/	شُ
/shā/	شى	/shin/	شٍ	/shī/	شي	/shi/	شِ

READ AND WRITE IT IN REAL CONTEXTS

Look at how ش is combined with other letters from the previous letter groups.

Find out what letters these words are composed of, join the combinations of letters as shown, then compare how the script is written in print and handwritten form.

Start with the main shape, then add the dots followed by the vowels.

Translation	Pronunciation	Handwriting practice	Combinations	Print form

←
Reading direction
Practise tracing the following and copy.

With long vowels

-	shā	‎_____ شا	ش ا	شا
-	shū	‎_____ شو	ش و	شو
-	shī	‎_____ شي	ش ي	شي

Insight

Known as المدينة الحمراء /al-madīnah al-ḥamrā'/ i.e. "the Red City",
Marrakech is becoming an increasingly famous tourist city in
Morocco, attracting visitors from all over the world. One of
the well-known tourist sites is جامع الفناء /jāmaᶜ al-fanā'/ known
in English as "Djemā el Fna", which is the largest traditional
market (سوق souk) and one of the busiest public squares in Africa
and the world.

وِلَاية مُرَاكُش

وِ ل ا يَ ة مُ رّ ا كُ ش

وِلَاية مُرَاكُش

wilāyat murrākush
Provence of Marrakech

Damascus	dimashq	دِمَشْق	دِ مَ شْ ق
apricot	mishmish	مِشْمِش	مِ شْ م ش
visa (section)	a(l)t-ta'shīrah	التَأشِيرَة	ال تَ أ شْ ي رَ ة
mosque	al-masjid	المَسْجِد	ال مَ سْ ج د

MOSQUE: PLEASE REMOVE SHOES

130

Insight

أَهْلاً وَسَهْلاً وَمَرْحَبًا

'ahlan wa sahlan wa marḥaban
Hello and welcome

This is another popular greeting expression Arabs use when welcoming someone to their home. The greeting was originally as follows, which was shortened later on:

حَلَلْتَ أَهْلاً وَنَزَلْتَ سَهْلاً

"You have stopped among your people and you have descended upon a plain"

Read aloud and practise writing the greeting first as individual words and then the whole greeting:

مَرْحَبًا	سَهْلاً	أَهْلاً
مَ رْ حَ ب أَ	سَ هْ ل أَ	أَ هْ ل أَ

أَهْلا _____

مَرْحَبًا _____	سَهْلا _____	
marḥaban	sahlan	ahlan
welcome	easy	family

أَهْلاً وَسَهْلاً وَمَرْحَبًا _____

إِنْ شَاءَ اللّٰه   شُكْرَأَ

| thank you | shukran | _____ | شُكْرَأَ | شُ كْ رَ أَ | شُكْرَأَ |
| if Allah wills | 'in shā' allah | _____ | إِنْ شَاءَ الله | إِنْ شَا ءَ اللّٰه | إِنْ شَاءَ الله |

(said when someone intends to do something in the future)

Insight

You already speak Arabic!

Here some more words that we use in English but that came originally from Arabic.

Syrup (lit. *beverage*) sharāb شَراب derived from the root word شرب sh-r-b i.e. to drink.

Artichoke, al-khurshūf الخُرْشوف is another word from Arabic that you probably know already!

Assassin (lit. *hashish users*) is an Arabic loanword derived from حَشاشين hashshāshīn, i.e. *hashish users*, which was also derived from the word حَشيش, i.e *hashish*. At the time of the Crusades, an Ismaili Shia sect had a reputation for murdering opposing leaders from Arabs and Crusaders after intoxicating themselves with hashish. This sect was known as حَشّاشين hashshāshīn.

ARABIC QUOTATION حِكْمَة عَرَبِيَّة

إِحْفَظْ قِرْشَكَ الأَبْيَضْ لِيَوْمِكَ الأَسْوَد

'ihfadh qirshaka al-'abyad liyawmika al-'aswad

Save your white penny for your black day
A penny saved is a penny earned
(idiomatic translation)

Arabic proverb

Circle the letters س ش wherever you see them in the quotation. Do you recognize any words that you have learned so far?

SUMMARY TABLE

The following table is a summary of what you need to know about the letters س ش.

Pronun-ciation	Joined up	Final	Medial	Initial	Isolated	Name
/s/ in seen	سسس	ـس	ـسـ	سـ	س	سين Sīn
/sh/ in sheep	ششش	ـش	ـشـ	شـ	ش	شين Shīn

Test yourself

Exercise 1
Read out loud and combine the letters to form words.

مِشْمِش   ا ل خَ م ي س   ا لخَمِيس   أ سْ وَ د

ا ل سَّ بْ ت   مُ رّا كُ ش   ا ل سّ و د ا ن

Exercise 2
Read out loud and write the unjoined forms of the letters that make up the following words.

سُكَّر   خَ مْ سَ ة   كُسْكُس   خَمْسَة

سِتَّة   دِمَشْق   تونِس

Exercise 3
Transliterate the words in Exercises 1 and 2 into roman script.

Exercise 4
Place the words in Exercises 1 and 2 into the right category.

Food	Countries and cities	Days	Public signs	Numbers	Colours

Exercise 5
What is the English equivalent of the following Arabic loanwords?

شَراب   حَشّاشين   الخُرْشوف

Exercise 6
Read the following expressions and translate into English. When do we usually say these expressions?

السَّلامُ عَلَيْكُم   أَهْلاً وَسَهْلا وَ مَرْحَبًا

شُكْراً   إنْ شاءَ الله

Exercise 7
Convert the following titles into the feminine.

سَيِّد   دُكْتور

Exercise 8
Read and translate the following public sign.

Unit 8

الوِحْدَة الثامِنَة

Letter group no. 8

Sād صاد
/s/

ص

Isolated

ـص   ـصـ   صـ

Final   Medial   Initial

Tā' طاء
/t/

ط

Isolated

ـط   ـطـ   طـ

Final   Medial   Initial

Dād ضاد
/d/

ض

Isolated

ـض   ـضـ   ضـ

Final   Medial   Initial

Dhā' ظاء
/dh/

ظ

Isolated

ـظ   ـظـ   ظـ

Final   Medial   Initial

In this unit you will learn
- **how to write and join the letters ص ض ط ظ**
- **how to read and recognize the letters in real contexts in a variety of script styles**
- **new and commonly used words**

The eighth letter group consists of four letters that share more or less the same skeleton shape and writing pattern, more specifically in the shape of an oval loop (ص). The only difference that distinguishes these letters is the number and location of dots, tails and strokes they carry.

Letter group no. 8 in a nutshell

Pronunciation	Joined up	Final	Medial	Initial	Isolated	Name
/s/ in sore	صصص	ـص	ـصـ	صـ	ص	صاد S̲ād
/d/ in doll	ضضض	ـض	ـضـ	ضـ	ض	ضاد D̲ād
/t/ in Spanish "tortilla"	ططط	ـط	ـطـ	طـ	ط	طاء T̲āʾ
dh	ظظظ	ـظ	ـظـ	ظـ	ظ	ظاء Dh̲āʾ

This group can be divided into two sub-groups.

Sub-group 1

The letters ض ص both share the same skeleton shape in all four positions. The shape is similar to an oval loop. The two letters are only dissimilar by a single dot, which is above the letter D̲āʾd ض. Another feature of this sub-group is that the tail is similar to that of ش س, but with a tiny hook after the loop (see table).

Pronunciation	Joined up	Final	Medial	Initial	Isolated	Name
/s/ in sore	صصص	ـص	ـصـ	صـ	ص	صاد S̲ād
/d/ in doll	ضضض	ـض	ـضـ	ضـ	ض	ضاد D̲ād

Sub-group 2

The letters ظ ط both share the skeleton shape of the main group in all positions (see table). The loop of ظ ط is identical to that of ض ص, with the following exceptions:

- Unlike the letters ض ص, they are written along the line.
- There is no hook after the loop.
- They don't have a tail.

Pronunciation	Joined up	Final	Medial	Initial	Isolated	Name
/t̲/ in Spanish 'tortilla'	ـططـ	ـط	ـطـ	طـ	ط	طاءٌ Ṭā'
/d̲h̲/	ـظظـ	ـظ	ـظـ	ظـ	ظ	ظاءٌ D̲h̲ā'

To illustrate the similarities between the four members of this letter group, compare the script in the different positions in the two tables we have just examined.

HOW TO WRITE IT

Skeleton shape

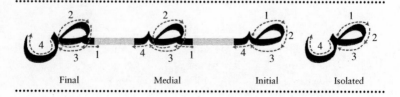

| Final | Medial | Initial | Isolated |

In the following activity, you will learn how to write the core skeleton shape of the letters ض ص and then ظ ط in the four different positions.

Then you will practise writing all these positions connected in one imaginary word.

Following the diagram, start with the main shape, and then add a vertical stroke followed by the dot above the letter.

Practise tracing the following and copy.

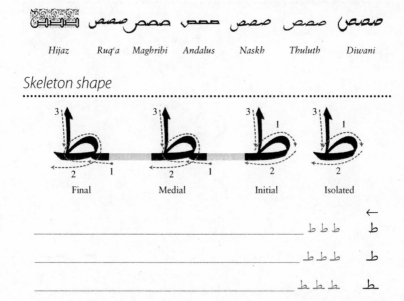

ص ص ص ← ص

ص ص ص ـصـ

ـصـ ـصـ ـصـ ـصـ

ـص ـص ـص ـص

صـصـ صـصـ صـصـ صـصـ صـصـ

Now, repeat the same writing exercise for the letter ض. Notice where the dot is positioned in the letter.

IN DIFFERENT CALLIGRAPHIC STYLES

This is how ص is written in different script and calligraphy styles. The letter Ḍād ض will look exactly the same, with the exception of a dot above.

| Hijaz | Ruqʻa | Maghribi | Andalus | Naskh | Thuluth | Diwani |

Skeleton shape

Final	Medial	Initial	Isolated

ط ط ط ← ط

ط ط ط ط

طـ طـ طـ طـ

ـط ط ط ط   ط

ـطـطـط ـطـطـط ـطـطـط ـطـطـط   ط ط ط

....

Now, repeat the same writing exercise for the letter ظ. Notice where the dot is positioned in the letter.

IN DIFFERENT CALLIGRAPHIC STYLES

This is how Ṭā' ط is written in different script and calligraphy styles. The letter Ḍād ظ will look exactly the same, with the exception of a dot above.

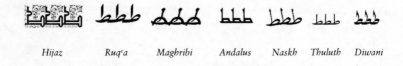

| Hijaz | Ruqʿa | Maghribi | Andalus | Naskh | Thuluth | Diwani |

_____

The letter Ṣād حَرْفُ الصّاد

Ṣād صاد
/ṣ/

ص

Isolated

ـص ـصـ صـ

Final Medial Initial

The first letter of this group is letter Ṣād صاد (ص), which is the fourteenth letter in the Arabic alphabet.

ص is a connector letter with four different shapes (ص صصص – see table).

Pronunciation	Joined up	Final	Medial	Initial	Isolated	Name
/s̱/ in sore	صصص	ـص	ـصـ	صـ	ص	صاد S̱ād

HOW TO READ IT

The letter S̱ād ص is one of the unfamiliar sounds in Arabic. It is pronounced like Sīn س , but with a deep emphatic /s̱/ as in the word s̱un, s̱ock and s̱ore.

ص is considered as the emphatic counterpart of Sīn س, hence transliterated as /s̱/, with a dash underneath to differentiate it from Sīn س /s/.

Emphatic consonants are always pronounced further back in the mouth than their frontal counterparts.

Do not confuse the two sounds Sīn س and S̱ād ص. Pay attention to how you pronounce the following similar sounding words.

/has̱ada/ to harvest	حَصَدَ	vs.	حَسَدَ	/hasada/ to envy

Notice how ص is sounded in combination with the different vowels and pronunciation symbols in the table.

Read the following letter/vowel combinations.

Supplementary vowels		Double vowels		Long vowels		Sort vowels	
/s̱s̱/	ضّ	/s̱an/	صاً	/s̱ā/	صا	/s̱a/	صَ
vowelless /s̱/	ضْ	/s̱un/	صٌّ	/s̱ū/	صو	/s̱u/	صُ
/s̱ā/	صى	/s̱in/	صٍ	/s̱ī/	صي	/s̱i/	صِ

Look at how ص is combined with other letters from the previous letter groups.

Find out what letters these words are composed of, join the combinations of letters as shown, then compare how the script is written in print and handwritten form.

Start with the main shape, then add the dots followed by the vowels.

Translation	Pronunciation	Handwriting practice	Combinations	Print form

←

Reading direction

Practise tracing the following and copy.

With long vowels

Translation	Pronunciation	Handwriting practice	Combinations	Print form
-	s̱ā	صا	ص ا	صا
-	s̱ū	صو	ص و	صو
-	s̱ī	صي	ص ي	صي
Egypt	mis̱r	مِصْر	م ص ر	مِصر
Somalia	a(l)s-s̱ūmāl	الصّومال	ا ل صّ و م ا ل	الصّومال
Sana'a	s̱anᶜā'	صَنْعاء	صَ نْ ع ا ء	صَنْعاء

QUICK VOCAB

Insight

So far, you have learned two common greeting expressions that you may use any time of the day. Do you still remember what they are?[1]

---

[1] السّلام عَلَيْكُم /a(l)-asalāmu ᶜalaikum/, i.e. Peace be upon you, and أَهْلاً وَسَهْلاً وَ مَرْحَبّا, i.e. hello and welcome.

How do you greet someone in Arabic in the morning, afternoon or evening?

Practise saying and writing the following greetings:

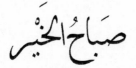

Good morning /ṣabāḥu al-khayr/ صَباحُ الخَير

صَباحُ الخَير _____ .

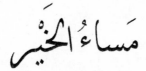

Good evening /masā'u al-khayr/ مَساءُ الخَير

مَساءُ الخَير _____ .

arrival	wuṣūl	وُصول _____	وُ ص و ل	وُصول
pharmacy	saydaliyyah	صَيْدَلِيَّة _____	صَ يْ دَ لِ يَّ ة	صَيْدَلِيَّة
subway	subwāy	صَبْ واي _____	صَ بْ و ا ي	صَبْ واي

The letter Ḍād حَرْفُ الضّاد

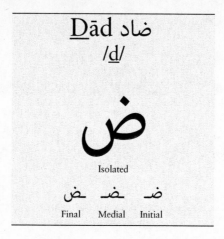

ضاد Ḍād
/ḍ/

ض

Isolated

ض ــضــ ـض

Final   Medial   Initial

The second letter of this group is letter Ḍād ضاد (ض), which is the fifteenth letter in the Arabic alphabet.

ض is a connector letter with four different shapes (ضضض ض - see table).

Pronunciation	Joined up	Final	Medial	Initial	Isolated	Name
ḍ	ضضض	ـض	ــضــ	ضــ	ض	ضاد Ḍād

HOW TO READ IT

The letter Ḍād (ض) is another emphatic sound in Arabic. It is pronounced like its emphatic counterpart Dāl (د), but deeper in the throat. The nearest equivalent sound in English is /d/ in the words *daunting* and *doll*.

It is transliterated as /d̲/, with a dash underneath to differentiate it from Dāl (د) /d/.

Do not confuse the two sounds D̲ād (ض) and Dāl (د). Pay attention to how you pronounce the following similar sounding examples.

/d̲alla/ to misguide s.o.	ضَلَّ	vs.	دَلَّ	/dalla/ to guide s.o.

Notice how ض is sounded in combination with the different vowels and pronunciation symbols in the table.

Read the following letter/vowel combinations.

Supplementary vowels		Double vowels		Long vowels		Short vowels	
/d̲d̲/	ضّ	/d̲an/	ضاً	/d̲ā/	ضا	/d̲a/	ضَ
vowelless /d̲/	ضْ	/d̲un/	ضٌ	/d̲ū/	ضو	/d̲u/	ضُ
/d̲ā/	ضى	/d̲in/	ضٍ	/d̲ī/	ضي	/d̲i/	ضِ

READ AND WRITE IT IN REAL CONTEXTS

Look at how ض is combined with other letters from the previous letter groups.

Find out what letters these words are composed of, join the combinations of letters as shown, then compare how the script is written in print and handwritten form.

Start with the main shape, then add the dots followed by the vowels.

Translation	Pronunciation	Handwriting practice	Combinations	Print form

←
Reading direction
Practise tracing the following and copy.

With long vowels

-	ḍā	_____ ضا	ض ا	ضا
-	ḍū	_____ ضو	ض و	ضو
-	ḍī	_____ ضي	ض ي	ضي

Colours

green (m.)	'akhḍar	_____ أخْضَر	أ خْ ضَ ر	أخْضَر
green (f.)	khaḍrā'	_____ خَضْراء	خَ ضْ ر ا ء	خَضْراء
white (m.)	'abyaḍ	_____ أبْيَض	أ بْ يَ ض	أبْيَض
white (f.)	bayḍā'	_____ بَيْضاء	بَ يْ ض ا ء	بَيْضاء
green Chinese tea	shāy sīniyy 'akhḍar	شاي صينيّ _____ أخْضَر	ش ا ي / ص ي نِ يّ / أ خْ ضَ ر	شاي / صينيّ / أخْضَر

What is the name of this green tea brand?

تويننجز من لندن

Insight

There are a variety of tea drinks in the Arabic culture. To say "tea with mint", you need to add the one-letter preposition بـ after شاي /shāy/:

Tea with ...	شاي بـ + ...
Tea with mint	شاي بالنعناع

How would you write the following in Arabic?

Tea with milk	....
Tea with sugar	....

Riyadh	a(l)r-riyād	الرِّياض _____ ا ل رِّ ي ا ض	الرِّياض

QUICK VOCAB

toilets	marāhīd	مَراحيض _____ مَ ر ا ح ي ض	مَراحيض
toilets	mirhād (singular form of مَراحيض)	مِرْحاض _____	مِرْحاض
toilets	dawratu al-miyāh	دَوْرَة المِياه _____	دَوْرَةُ المِياه

الدَّيكُ الفَصِيح مِنْ داخِلِ البَيْضَةِ يَصِيح

a(l)d-dīk al-faṣīḥ min dākhil al-bayḍa yaṣīḥ
An eloquent rooster crows within its egg shell

Arabic proverb

Circle the letters ض ص wherever you see them in the quotation.
Do you recognize any familiar words in the quotation that you
have learned so far?

The letter Ṭāʾ حَرْفُ الطَّاء

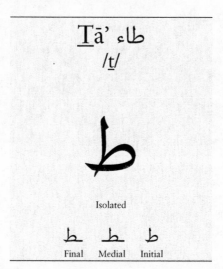

Ṭāʾ طاء
/ṭ/

ط

Isolated

ط   ط   ط
Final Medial Initial

The third letter of this group is letter Ṭāʾ طاء (ط), which is the
fifteenth letter in the Arabic alphabet.

ط is a connector letter with four different shapes (ططط ط – see table).

Pronunciation	Joined up	Final	Medial	Initial	Isolated	Name
/ṭ/ in spanish 'tortilla'	ططط	ـط	ـطـ	طـ	ط	طاء Ṭā'

HOW TO READ IT

The letter Ṭā' (ط) is another unfamiliar sound in Arabic. It is the phonetic emphatic counterpart of Tā' (ت) pronounced further back in the mouth.

It is pronounced as /ṭ/ as in the Spanish dish *tortilla de patatas*.

It is transliterated as /ṭ/ with a dash to differentiate it from Tā' (ت).

Do not confuse the two sounds Tā' (ت) and Ṭā' (ط). Pay attention to how you pronounce the following similar sounding examples.

/ṭayyār/ pilot	طَيّار	vs.	تَيّار	/tayyār/ flow, stream

Notice how the letter Ṭā' (ط) is sounded in combination with the different vowels and pronunciation symbols in the table.

Read the following letter/vowel combinations.

Supplementary vowels		Double vowels		Long vowels		Short vowels	
/ṭṭ/	طّ	/ṭan/	طًا	/ṭā/	طا	/ṭa/	طَ
vowelless /ṭ/	طْ	/ṭun/	طٌ	/ṭū/	طو	/ṭu/	طُ
/ṭā/	طى	/ṭin/	طٍ	/ṭī/	طي	/ṭi/	طِ

READ AND WRITE IT IN REAL CONTEXTS

Look at how ط is combined with other letters from the previous letter groups.

Find out what letters these words are composed of, join the combinations of letters as shown, then compare how the script is written in print and handwritten form.

Start with the main shape, then add the dots followed by the vowels.

Translation	Pronunciation	Handwriting practice	Combinations	Print form

←
Reading direction
Practise tracing the following and copy.

With long vowels

-	ṭā	ـــــــــــ طا	ط ا	طا
-	ṭū	ـــــــــــ طو	ط و	طو
-	ṭī	ـــــــــــ طي	ط ي	طي

potatoes	baṭāṭā	ـــــــــــ بَطاطا	بَ ط ا ط ا	بطاطا
tomatoes	ṭamāṭim	ـــــــــــ طَماطِم	طَ م ا طِ م	طَماطِم

QUICK VOCAB

طماطم كاتشب

150

English	Transliteration	(blank)	Arabic	Arabic letters
doctor (medical)	ṭabīb	طَبيب	طَبيب	طَ ب ي ب
sick, patient	marīḍ	مَريض	مَريض	مَ ر ي ض
Mauritania	mūrītānyā	موريطانيا	موريطانيا	م و ر ي ط ا ن ي ا
Tripoli	ṭarāblus	طَرابلُس	طَرابلُس	طَ ر ا بْ لُ س
Khartoum[1]	al-khurṭūm	الخُرطوم	الخُرطوم	ا ل خُ رْ ط و م
Italy	'īṭālyā	إيطاليا	إيطاليا	إ ي ط ا ل ي ا
Britain	'brīṭāniyā	إبريطانيا	إبريطانيا	إ بْ ر ي ط ا نْ ي ا
police	a(l)sh-shurṭah	الشُّرطَة	الشُّرطَة	ا ل شُّ ر ط ة
Rabat[2]	a(l)r-rabāṯ	الرّباط	الرّباط	ا ل رِّ ب ا ط
airport	maṭār	مَطار	مَطار	مَ ط ا ر
danger	khaṯar	خَطَر	خَطَر	خَ طَ ر

[1]Capital of Sudan.
[2]Capital of المغرب /al-maghrebl/ i.e. Morocco.

طَبِيبٌ يُداوِي النّاسَ وَهُوَ مَرِيض

ṭabībun yudāwī a(l)n-nāsa wa huwa marīḏ
Like a physician curing the people while he himself is distempered

Arabic proverb

Circle the letters ط ض wherever you see them in the quotation.
Do you recognize in the quotation any familiar words that you
have learned so far?

The letter Dhā' حَرْفُ الظّاء

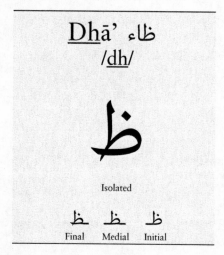

Dhā' ظاء
/dh/

ظ

Isolated

ظ   ظ   ظ
Final   Medial   Initial

The last letter of this group is letter Dhā' ظاء (ظ), which is the
sixteenth letter in the Arabic alphabet.

ظ is a connector letter with four different shapes (ظظظ ظ – see table).

Pronunciation	Joined up	Final	Medial	Initial	Isolated	Name
<u>dh</u>	ظظظ	ظ	ظ	ظ	ظ	<u>Dh</u>ā' ظاء

HOW TO READ IT

The letter <u>Dh</u>ā' ظ is another unfamiliar and tricky sound in Arabic. It is pronounced like its emphatic counterpart Dhāl ذ /dh/, but more deeply from the throat.

Due to the difficulty in pronunciation, it is also commonly pronounced as ز /z/ or the empathic ض /<u>d</u>/.

ظ is transliterated as /<u>dh</u>/ with a dash to differentiate it from Dhāl ذ /dh/.

Do not confuse the two sounds Dhāl (ذ) and <u>Dh</u>ā' (ظ). Pay attention to how you pronounce the following similar sounding examples.

/<u>dh</u>alīl/ shaded	ظَليل	vs.	ذَليل	/dhalīl/ despicable

Notice how the letter <u>Dh</u>ā' ظ is sounded in combination with the different vowels and pronunciation symbols in the table.

Read the following letter/vowel combinations.

Supplementary vowels		Double vowels		Long vowels		Short vowels	
/<u>dh</u>dh/	ظّ	/<u>dh</u>an/	ظًا	/<u>dh</u>ā/	ظا	/<u>dh</u>a/	ظَ
vowelless /<u>dh</u>/	ظْ	/<u>dh</u>un/	ظٌ	/<u>dh</u>ū/	ظو	/<u>dh</u>u/	ظُ
/<u>dh</u>ā/	ظى	/<u>dh</u>in/	ظٍ	/<u>dh</u>ī/	ظي	/<u>dh</u>i/	ظِ

READ AND WRITE IT IN REAL CONTEXTS

Look at how ظ is combined with other letters from the previous letter groups.

Find out what letters these words are composed of, join the combinations of letters as shown, then compare how the script is written in print and handwritten form.

Start with the main shape, then add the dots followed by the vowels.

Translation	Pronunciation	Handwriting practice	Combinations	Print form

←

Reading direction

Practise tracing the following and copy.

With long vowels

-	<u>dh</u>ā	ظا	ظ ا	ظا
-	<u>dh</u>ū	ظو	ظ و	ظو
-	<u>dh</u>ī	ظي	ظ ي	ظي

back	<u>dh</u>ahr	ظَهْر	ظ هْ ر	ظَهْر
noon	<u>dh</u>uhr	ظُهْر	ظ هْ ر	ظُهْر
afternoon	ba'da <u>dhdh</u>uhr	بَعْدَ الظُّهْر	بَ عْ دَ ا ل ظُّ هْ ر	بَعْدَ الظُّهْر
luck	ha<u>dhdh</u>	حَظّ	حَ ظّ	حَظّ
lucky	ma<u>hdh</u>ūdh	مَحظوظ	مَ حْ ظ و ظ	مَحْظوظ

154

أَبوظَبي

أ ب و ظَ ب ي

أبوظبي

Can you figure out which Arab city this car registration plate belongs to?

PLEASE KEEP THE PLACE CLEAN AND TIDY

الرَّجاء المُحافَظة عَلى النِّظام والنَّظافة

ال رَّ ج اء ا ل مُ ح ا فَ ظ ة عَ ل ى ا ل نِّ ظ ا م وَ ا ل نَّ ظ ا فَ ة

a(l)r-rajā' al-muḥāfaḍha ʿalā a(l)n-niḍhām wa a(l)n-naḏhāfah
Please keep the place tidy and clean

Circle the letters you have learned so far.
How many times do they occur in this sign?

Do you recognize any familiar words in the sign?

حافِظوا عَلى نَظافة المَدينة

ح ا ف ِ ظ و ا عَ ل ى نَ ظ ا فَ ة ا ل مَ د ي نَ ة

hāfidhū halā nadhāfat al-madīnah
Keep the city clean

Insight

You already speak Arabic!

Gibraltar /jabal ṯāriq/ جَبَل طارق, a British overseas territory since 1704, was conquered in 710 CE by a Muslim leader named Tarik Ibn Ziyad طارق ابن زياد, from whom the mountain was named.

It literally means "the mountain of Tarik".

Mattress ma<u>t</u>ra<u>h</u> مَطْرَح was originally borrowed in Sicily from Arabic, and derived from the root word <u>t</u>-r-<u>h</u> i.e. to throw down. The literal meaning of mattress is "is the thing thrown down".

صَحْراء

صَ خْ ر ا ء

صَحْراء

sahrā'

Sahara

The great African desert, the Sahara, another Arabic loanword.

SUMMARY TABLE

The following table is a summary of what you need to know about the letters ص ض ط ظ.

Pronunciation	Joined up	Final	Medial	Initial	Isolated	Name	
<u>s</u>	صصص	ـص	ـصـ	صـ	ص	صاد	<u>S</u>ād
<u>d</u>	ضضض	ـض	ـضـ	ضـ	ض	ضاد	<u>D</u>ād
<u>t</u>	ططط	ـط	ـطـ	طـ	ط	طاء	<u>T</u>ā'
<u>dh</u>	ظظظ	ـظ	ـظـ	ظـ	ظ	ظاء	<u>Dh</u>ā'

Test yourself

Exercise 1
Read out loud and combine the letters to form words.

أ ب و ظَ ب ي   مَ ر ا ح ي ض   شاي   ش ا ي

ا ل شُّ ر ط ة   ا ل رِّ ب ا ط   طَ م ا طِ م

Exercise 2
Read out loud and write the unjoined forms of the letters that
make up the following words.

مَطار   بَ ط ا ط ا   أَخْضَر   بَطاطا

أَبْيَض   خَطَر   موريطانيا

Exercise 3
Transliterate the words in Exercises 1 and 2 into roman script.

Exercise 4
Place the words in Exercises 1 and 2 into the right category.

Food	Countries and cities	Public signs	Numbers	Colours

Exercise 5
What are the English equivalents of the following Arabic loanwords?

مَطْرَح   صَحْراء   جَبَل طارق

Exercise 6
Read the following expressions and translate into English. When do we usually say these expressions? Put them into chronological order of their use.

مَساءُ الخَير   صَباحُ الخَير   بَعْدَ الظُّهْر

Exercise 7
Convert the following titles into the feminine.

طَبِيب   مَرِيض

Exercise 8
Read and translate the text in the following packaging.

العلامة = label

Exercise 9

Do you recognize the name of this famous Moroccan city?

(Hint: If translated literally, it reads "White House".)

Unit 9

Letter group no. 9

ᶜayn عَين
/ᶜ/

Ghayn غَين
/gh/

ع

Isolated

ح ـعـ عـ

Final   Medial   Initial

غ

Isolated

ـغ ـغـ غـ

Final   Medial   Initial

In this unit you will learn
- *how to write and join the letters* ع غ
- *how to read and recognize the letters in real contexts in a variety of script styles*
- *new and commonly used words*

The ninth letter group is a unique group. It has only two letters that share one distinguished core letter shape (ع), one of which has a distinctive sound unique to Arabic غ and arguably the most complicated one to articulate: the letter ᶜayn (ع). The two letters are: ᶜayn عَين (ع) and Ghayn غَين (غ) in alphabetical order.

The tail of both letters (ع غ) is similar to a half-closed circle that dips below the line. In fact, it is exactly identical to that of the letter group (ج ح خ) in Unit 6. Also, in writing the script, the only minor difference between the two letters is a single dot above Ghayn (غ) غَين, while ayn عَين (ع) has no dots at all.

Pronunciation	Joined up	Final	Medial	Initial	Isolated	Name
/ᶜ/ in French 'Paris'	ععع	ع	ـعـ	عـ	ع	عَيْـن ᶜayn
/gh/	غغغ	غ	ـغـ	غـ	غ	غَيْـن Ghayn

HOW TO WRITE IT

Skeleton shape

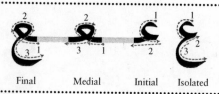

| Final | Medial | Initial | Isolated |

In the following activity, you will learn how to write the core shape of the letters ع غ in the four different positions.

Then you will practise writing all these positions connected in one imaginary word.

Following the diagram of the skeleton shape, practise tracing the following and copy.

←

	ععع	ع
	ـعـ ـعـ ـعـ	ـعـ
	ـعـ ـعـ ـعـ	ـعـ
	ععع	عـ
	ععع ععع ععع	ععـ

Now, repeat the same writing exercise for the letter غ. Notice where the dot is positioned in the letter.

IN DIFFERENT CALLIGRAPHIC STYLES

This is how ع is written in different script and calligraphy styles. The letter غ will look exactly the same, with the exception of a dot above it.

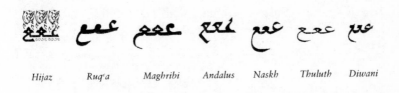

| Hijaz | Ruq'a | Maghribi | Andalus | Naskh | Thuluth | Diwani |

The letter ʿayn حَرْفُ العَين

ʿayn عَين
/ʿ/

ع

Isolated

ع ـعـ ـع
Final Medial Initial

The first letter of this group is ʿayn عَين (ع), which is the eighteenth letter in the Arabic alphabet.

ع is a connector letter with four different shapes (ععع ع – see table.)

Pronun- ciation	Joined up	Final	Medial	Initial	Isolated		Name
/ᶜ/	ععع	ـع	ـعـ	عـ	ع	عَيْن	ᶜayn

HOW TO READ IT

Here we come to the most unique and distinctive sound in Arabic, yet arguably the most complicated one to articulate: ᶜayn ع.

ع ᶜayn is another Arabic letter that has no equivalent in European languages. It is pronounced as a guttural sound deeper from the throat. To be able to produce such a sound, try to say /ah/ deep from your stomach, as if you were being strangled! Another nearer sound is that of Ḥā' ح /ḥ/, which is considered a voiceless counterpart of ᶜayn ع.

ᶜayn ع is transliterated with a superscript letter c / ᶜ/ to illustrate the beginning of ع. Sometimes, you might find it transliterated as number 3 (reverse ع) or as an apostrophe /'/. In this book, we are using /'/ for the consonant Alif أ and /ᶜ/ for ᶜayn.

Notice how ع is sounded in combination with the different vowels and pronunciation symbols in the table.

Make sure you do not confuse the sounds of the ᶜayn ع with Ḥā' ح or Alif أ.

Now, pay attention to how you pronounce the following similar sounding examples.

| /'amal/ hope | أَمَل | | | |
| /ḥamal/ lamb (unholy) | حَمَل | vs. | عَمَل | /ᶜamal/ labour |

Read the following letter/vowel combinations, working from right to left.

Supplementary vowels		Double vowels		Long vowels		Short vowels	
/ᶜᶜ/	غّ	/ᶜan/	عًا	/ᶜā/	عا	/ᶜa/	عَ
vowelless /ᶜ/	غْ	/ᶜun/	عٌ	/ᶜū/	عو	/ᶜu/	عُ
/ᶜā/	عى	/ᶜin/	عٍ	/ᶜī/	عي	/ᶜi/	عِ

READ AND WRITE IT IN REAL CONTEXT

Look at how ع is combined with other letters from the previous letter groups.

Find out what letters these words are composed of, join the combinations of letters as shown, then compare how the script is written in print and handwritten form.

Start with the main shape, then add the dots followed by the vowels.

Translation	Pronunciation	Handwriting practice	Combinations	Print form
		←		

Reading direction
Practise tracing the following and copy.

With long vowels

-	ᶜā	_____ عا	ا ع	عا
-	ᶜū	_____ عو	ع و	عو
-	ᶜī	_____ عي	ع ي	عي

about	ʿan	_____ عَن	عَ ن	عَن
above, on	ʿalā	_____ عَلى	عَ ل ى	عَلى
at	ʿinda	_____ عِنْدَ	عِ نْ دَ	عِنْدَ
paternal uncle	ʿamm	_____ عَمَ	عَ مّ	عَمّ
paternal aunt	ʿammah	_____ عَمَّة	عَ مّ ة	عَمَّة

Days of the week

| Friday | al-jumuʿah | _____ الجُمعَة | ا ل جُ مُ عَ ة | الجُمَعة |
| Wednesday | al-'arbiʿā' | _____ الأَربِعاء | ا ل أ ر بِ ع ا ء | الأَربِعاء |

Numbers

So far you have learned the numbers one, two, three, five, six and eight. Here are the remaining numbers up to ten, and their compounds, most of which are spelled with the letter ع.

	4	'arbaʿah	_____ أَربَعة	أ ر بَ عَ ة	أَربَعة
٤	40	'arbaʿūn	_____ أَربَعون	أ ر بَ ع و ن	أَربَعون
	4th	a(l)r-rābiʿ/ah	_____ الرّابِع	ا ل رّ ا بِ ع	الرّابِع/ة
	1/4	rubuʿ	_____ رُبع	رُ بُ ع	رُبع
	7	sabʿah	_____ سَبعة	سَ بْ عَ ة	سَبعة
	70	sabʿūn	_____ سَبعون	سَ بْ ع و ن	سَبعون
٧	7th	a(l)s-sabiʿ/ah	_____ السّابِع	ا ل سّ ا بِ ع	السّابِع/ة
	1/7	subuʿ	_____ سُبع	سُ بُ ع	سُبع

	9	tisᶜah	تِسعَة	ت سْ عَ ة	تِسْعَة
٩	90	tisᶜūn	تِسعون	ت سْ ع و ن	تِسْعون
	9th	a(l)t-tāsiᶜ/ah	التَّاسِع	ا ل تَّ اس ع	التَّاسِع /ة
	1/9	tusuᶜ	تُسع	تُ سُ ع	تُسْع
	10	ᶜasharah	عَشَرَة	عَ شَ رَ ةٌ	عَشَرَةٌ
١٠	1/10	ᶜushur	عُشر	عُ شُ ر	عُشر
	10	al-ᶜāshir/ah	العاشِر/ة	ا ل ع ا شِ ر /ة	العاشِر/ة

Happy New Year Lit. May you (and your family) be well every year	kullu ᶜaamin wa 'antum bikhayr	كُلُّ عَامٍ وَأَنْتم بِخَير	كُلُّ عَامٍ وَأَنْتم بِخَير

Al-Zuhour Street (lit. roses)	shāriᶜ a(l)z-zuhūr	شارع الزُهور	شا رِ ع ا ل ز ه و ر	(شارِع) (الزُهور)

NOTICE BOARD

Notice board	lawahat al-i ᶜlānāt	لَوْحَة الإغلانات	لَ وْ حَ ة ا ل إ غْ ل ا ن ا ت	لَوْحة الإغلانات

Restaurant   maṭ‘am   _____   مَطْعَم   مَ طْ عَ م   مَطْعَم

مَطْعَم روبس – مَطْبَخ دُوَلِيّ

مَ طْ عَ م روبس – مَ طْ بَ خ دُ وَ لِ يّ

مَطْعَم روبس — مَطْبَخ دُوَلِيّ

maṭ‘am ruubis – maṭbakh duwaliyy

Rubis Restaurant – international cuisine

عافية

ع ا ف ِ يَ ة

عافية _____

رَقْم ١ في العالَم العَرَبي

رَ قْ م ١ ف ي ا ل ع ا لَ م ا ل عَ رَ بِ ي

رَقْم ١ في العالَم العَرَبي _____

raqm wāhid fī al-‘ālam al-‘arabiyy

Number one in the Arab world

| No
smoking | mamnū^c
a(l)t-tadkhīn | مَمْنوع
التَّدْخين | مَ مْ ن و ع
ال تَّ دْ خ
ي ن | مَمْنوع التَّدْخين |

مَمْنوع الدُّخول

مَ مْ ن و ع ال دُّ خ و ل

مَمْنوع الدُّخول _____

mamnū^c a(l)d-dukhūl

No admittance

مَمْنوع وُقوف السَّيّارات

مَ مْ ن و ع وُ ق و ف ال سَّ يّ ا ر ات

مَمْنوع وُقوف السَّيّارات

_____

mamnū^c wuqūf a(l)s-sayyārāt

No parking (of vehicles)

Arbic names

Ali	ᶜalī	_____ عَلِيّ	عَ لِ يّ	عَلِيّ
Omar	ᶜomar	_____ عُمَر	عُ مَ ر	عُمَر
servant of Allāh	ᶜabdullāh	_____ عَبْدُ الله	عَ بْ دُ ا ل ه	عَبْدُ الله

The letter Ghayn حَرْفُ الغَين

Ghayn غَين
/gh/

غ

Isolated

غ   غ   غـ
Final   Medial   Initial

The second letter of this group is letter Ghayn غَيْـن (غ), which is the nineteenth letter in the Arabic alphabet.

غ is a connector letter with four different shapes (غ غغغ – see table.)

Pronunciation	Joined up	Final	Medial	Initial	Isolated	Name
/gh/ in French 'paris'	غغغ	غ	ـغـ	غـ	غ	غَيْن Ghayn

HOW TO READ IT

The nearest sound to the letter Ghayn غ is that of gargling. It is also similar to that of Khā' خ /kh/ which, along with غ, both come from the same place of articulation in your vocal system. However, غ is more vocal and pronounced as /r/ in French "Paris" or "rouge". غ is typically transliterated as /gh/.

Do not confuse the two sounds Ghayn غ and Khā' خ. Pay attention to how you pronounce the following similar sounding examples:

/raghwah / froth	رَغْوَة	vs.	رَخْوَة	/ rakhwah / loose

Notice how غ is sounded in combination with the different vowels and pronunciation symbols in the table.

Read the following letter/vowel combinations.

Supplementary vowels		Double vowels		Long vowels		Short vowels	
/ghgh/	غْ	/ghan/	غًا	/ghā/	غا	/gha/	غَ
vowelless /gh/	غْ	/ghun/	غٌ	/ghū/	غو	/ghu/	غُ
/ghā/	غى	/ghin/	غٍ	/ghī/	غي	/ghi/	غِ

READ AND WRITE IT IN REAL CONTEXTS

Look at how غ is combined with other letters from the previous letter groups.

Find out what letters these words are composed of, join the combinations of letters as shown, then compare how the script is written in print and handwritten form.

Start with the main shape, then add the dots followed by the vowels.

Translation	Pronunciation	Handwriting practice	Combinations	Print form

←

Reading direction

Practise tracing the following and copy.

With long vowels

-	ghā	غا _____	غ ا	غا
-	ghū	غو_____	غ و	غو
-	ghī	غي_____	غ ي	غي

Insight

Arab vs. Western world

There is an immense difference between the Arab world and the West in all walks of life: in language, culture, traditions, lifestyle, and people. Yet, linguistically in Arabic, the equivalent of "Arabs" and "West" is almost identical in writing and can be easily confused for homographs (i.e. similar in spelling but different in meaning). The only minor difference between the two words is a single dot!

Arab (people)	ᶜarab	عَرَب _____	عَ رَ ب	عَرَب
Arab (adj. or noun) m./f.	ᶜarabiyy /ah	عَرَبيّ /ة_____	عَ رَ بِ يّ / ة	عَرَبيّ/ة
Arabic (language)	al-ᶜarabiyyah	العَرَبِيّة_____	ا ل عَ رَ بِ يّ ة	العَرَبِيّة
Arabist	mustaᶜrab	مُسْتَعْرَب_____	مُ سْ تَ عْ رَ ب	مُسْتَعْرَب

Al Arabiya News Channel

Logo of the Arabic channel al-Arabiya

west (direction)	gharb	غَرْب _____	غَ رْ ب	غَرْب
the West	al-gharb	الغَرْب _____	ا ل غَ رْ ب	الغَرْب
Western m./f.	gharbiyy/ah	غَرْبي /ة _____	غَ رْ ب ي / ة	غَرْبي/ة
sunset	ghrūb	غروب _____	غُ ر و ب	غُروب

the Bank of Morocco	bank al-maghreb	بَنْك المَغْرِب _____	بَ نْ ك ا ل مَ غْ رِ ب	بَنْك المَغْرِب
Moroccan[1]	maghrebiyyah	مَغْرِبي /ة _____	مَ غْ رِ ب ي / ة	مَغْرِبي/ة
Baghdad	baghdād	بَغْداد _____	بَ غْ د ا د	بَغْداد

| Oman | ᶜummān | عُمان _____ | عُ م ا ن | عُمان |

---

[1] Lit. "the place when the sun sets". المَغْرِب is also one of the daily five prayers in Islam performed at sunset.

ARABIC QUOTATION حِكْمَة عَرَبيَّة

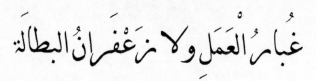

غُبَارُ الْعَمَلِ ولا زَعْفِرانُ البِطالَةِ

ghubāru al-ᶜamal walā zaᶜ faran al-biṭāala
The dust of work (is better) than the saffron of joblessness

Arabic proverb

Circle the letters (ع غ) wherever you see them in the quotation.
Do you recognize any familiar words in the quotation that you
have learned so far?

SUMMARY TABLE

The following table is a summary of what you need to know about
the letters ع غ.

Pronun-ciation	Joined up	Final	Medial	Initial	Isolated		Name
ᶜ	ععع	ع	ـعـ	عـ	ع	عَيْن	ᶜayn
gh	غغغ	غ	ـغـ	غـ	غ	غَيْن	Ghayn

Test yourself

Exercise 1
Read out loud and combine the letters to form words.

عَ شَ رَ ة   ا ل جُ مُ عَ ة   شا ر ع

أ ر ب عَ ة   ا ل أ ر ب عا ء   ا ل مَ غْ ر ب

Exercise 2

Read out loud and write the unjoined forms of the letters that make up the following words.

مَطْعَم   بَغْداد   سَ بْ عَ ة   سَبْعَة

عَبْدُ الله   تِسْعَة   عُمان

Exercise 3

Transliterate the words in Exercises 1 and 2 into roman script.

Exercise 4

Place the words in Exercises 1 and 2 into the right category.

Days	Countries	Cities	Public signs	Numbers	Arabic names

Exercise 5

Match the following warning public signs with their correct Arabic text.

مَمْنوع التَّدْخين	No parking
مَمْنوع الدُّخول	No smoking
مَمْنوع وُقوف السَّيّارات	No entry

Exercise 6

List a minimum of two derivative words of عرب and غرب.

Exercise 7

Put the following days of the week into chronological order from Sunday to Saturday.

الأَرْبِعاء   الإثْنَيْن   السَّبْت   الثُّلاثاء   الأَحَد   الجُمْعَة   الخَميس

Unit **10**

....

Letter group no. 10

Fā' فاء
/f/

Qāf قاف
/q/

ف

Isolated

ف ـف ـف
Final Medial Initial

ق

Isolated

ق ـقـ قـ
Final Medial Initial

In this unit you will learn
- *how to write and join the letters ق ف*
- *how to read and recognize the letters in real contexts in a variety of script styles*
- *new and commonly used words*

And so we come to the last letter group of the Arabic alphabet. Similarly to the previous one, there are only two letters in this group. They are both identical in shape but only in the initial and medial positions with minor differences in the isolated and final positions.

The two letters are: Fā' فاء (ف) and Qāf قاف (ق) in alphabetical order.

The shape of ف is similar to a wide kayak, exactly like the letters of the second group (ب ت ث).

Unlike ف, the letter ق has two dots above with a semi-circle rounded tail that goes deep below the line (like س, ش, ض, ص). ف is written above the line as is the case with ب ت ث.

Letter group no. 10 in a nutshell

Pronunciation	Joined up	Final	Medial	Initial	Isolated	Name	
/f/ in five	ففف	ـف	ـفـ	فـ	ف	فاء	Fā'
/q/	ققق	ـق	ـقـ	قـ	ق	قاف	Qāf

HOW TO WRITE IT

Skeleton shape

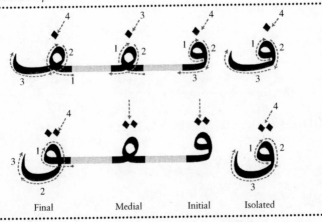

| Final | Medial | Initial | Isolated |

In the following activity, you will learn how to write the core shape of the letters ف ق in the four different positions. Then you will practise writing all these positions connected in one imaginary word.

Following the diagram of the skeleton shapes, practise tracing the following and copy.

←

ف   ف ف ف

ف   ف ف ف

ف   ف ف ف

Now, repeat the same exercise for the letter ق.

Notice where the two dots are positioned.

Final form of each letter

ف   ف ف ف

ق   ق ق ق

Connect the three forms in one imaginary word.

ف ف ف   ففف ففف ففف

ققق   ققق ققق ققق

IN DIFFERENT CALLIGRAPHIC STYLES

ففف   ففف   ففف   ففف   ففف   ففف   ففف

ققق   ققق   ققق   ققق   ققق   ققق   ققق

Hijaz   Ruq'a   Maghribi   Andalus   Naskh   Thuluth   Diwani

178

The letter Fā' حَرْفُ الفاء

Fā' فاء
/f/

ف

Isolated

ف ﻔ ﻓ
Final Medial Initial

The first letter of this group is Fā' فاء (ف), which is the twentieth letter in the Arabic alphabet.

ف is a connector letter with four different shapes (ف فف – see table).

Pronunciation	Joined up	Final	Medial	Initial	Isolated	Name
f	فف	ف	ـفـ	ف	ف	فاء Fā'

HOW TO READ IT

The letter Fā' ف is an easy letter to read and its sound exists in most world languages. It is transliterated and pronounced as /f/ as in the word *five*, *fine* or *fork*. The proper name of the letter Fā' فاء is coincidentally very similar to the English word *fat* pronounced with a silent t.

Notice how ف is sounded in combination with the different vowels and pronunciation symbols in the table.

Read the following letter/vowel combinations.

Supplementary vowels		Double vowels		Long vowels		Short vowels	
/ff/	فّ	/fan/	فًا	/fā/	فا	/fa/	فَ
vowelless /f/	فْ	/fun/	فٌ	/fū/	فو	/fu/	فُ
/fā/	فى	/fin/	فٍ	/fī/	في	/fi/	فِ

READ AND WRITE IT IN REAL CONTEXTS

Look at how ف is combined with other letters from the previous letter groups.

Find out what letters these words are composed of, join the combinations of letters as shown, then compare how the script is written in print and handwritten form.

Start with the main shape, then add the dots followed by the vowels.

Translation	Pronunciation	Handwriting practice	Combinations	Print form

←
Reading direction
Practise tracing the following and copy.

With long vowels

-	fā	_____ فا	ف ا	فا
-	fū	_____ فو	ف و	فو
-	fī	_____ في	ف ي	في

beans	fūl	فول	ف و ل	فول
falafel	falāfil	فَلافِل	فَ ل ا فِ ل	فَلافِل
yellow (m.)	'aṣfar	أصفَر	أ صْ فَ ر	أَصْفَر
yellow (f.)	ṣafrā'	صَفْراء	صَ فْ ر اء	صَفْراء
Palestine for the Arabs	filasṭīn lil ᶜarab	فِلَسْطين	فِ لَ سْ ط ي ن لْ لْ عَ رَ ب	فِلَسْطين لِلْعَرَب
public phone	hātif ᶜumūmiyy	هاتِف غُمومِي	ه ا تِ ف عُ مْ و مِ ي	هاتِف غُموِمي

Letter group no. 10 181

The letter Qāf حَرْفُ القاف

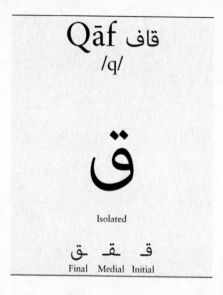

Qāf قاف
/q/

ق

Isolated

ق ــقـ ــق
Initial Medial Final

The second letter of this group is letter Qāf (ق), which is the twenty-first letter in the Arabic alphabet.

ق is a connector letter with four different shapes (ق ققق – see table).

Pronunciation	Joined up	Final	Medial	Initial	Isolated	Name
/q/	ققق	ــق	ــقـ	ق	ق	قاف Qāf'

HOW TO READ IT

The sound of letter Qāf (ق) has no equivalent in any European language. ق is actually the emphatic counterpart of Kāf ك /k/, but pronounced further back in the throat, as if you were drowning.

It is usually dropped in spoken Arabic (particularly in Egypt and the Levant) and pronounced as Alif.

Qāf (ق) is typically transliterated with the letter /q/.

Do not confuse the two sounds Qāf (ق) and Kāf كـ. Pay attention to how you pronounce the following similar sounding examples:

/kalb/ dog	كَلْب		قَلْب	/qalb/ heart
		vs.		
/rakīk/ prosaic	رَكيك		رَقيق	/raqīq/ thin

Notice how ق is sounded in combination with the different vowels and pronunciation symbols in the table.

Read the following letter/vowel combinations.

Supplementary vowels		Double vowels		Long vowels		Short vowels	
/qq/	قّ	/qan/	قًا	/qā/	قا	/qa/	قَ
vowelless /q/	قْ	/qun/	قٌ	/qū/	قو	/qu/	قُ
/qā/	قى	/qin/	قٍ	/qī/	قي	/qi/	قِ

READ AND WRITE IT IN REAL CONTEXTS

Look at how ق is combined with other letters from the previous letter groups.

Find out what letters these words are composed of, join the combinations of letters as shown, then compare how the script is written in print and handwritten form.

Start with the main shape, then add the dots followed by the vowels.

Translation	Pronunciation	Handwriting practice	Combinations	Print form

←
Reading direction
Practise tracing the following and copy.

With long vowels

	qā	قا	ق ا	قا
	qū	قو	ق و	قو
	qī	قي	ق ي	قي

how	kayfa	كَيْفَ	كَ يْ فَ	كَيْفَ
above	fawqa	فَوْقَ	فَ وْ قَ	فَوْقَ
before*	qabla	قَبْلَ	ق بْ لَ	قَبْلَ
coffee	qahwah	قَهْوَة	قْ هْ وَ ة	قَهْوَة
wheat flour	daqīq	دَقيق	دَ ق ي ق	دَقيق
blue (m.)	'azraq	أزْرَق	أ زْ رَ ق	أزْرَق
blue (f.)	zarqā'	زَرْقاء	زَ رْ ق ا ء	زَرْقاء
oranges	burtuqāl	بُرْتُقال	بُ رْ تُ ق ا ل	بُرْتُقال
orange (colour)	burtuqāliyy	بُرْتُقالِيّ	بُ رْ تُ ق ا لِ يّ	بُرْتُقالِيّ
Qatar	qaṭar	قَطَر	قَ طَ ر	قَطَر
Iraq	al-ʿirāq	العِراق	ا ل عِ ر ا ق	العِراق
Cairo	al-qāhirah	القاهِرَة	ا ل ق ا هِ رَ ة	القاهِرَة

QUICK VOCAB

---

* For instance, if you wish to say "before noon" it would be قَبْلَ الظُهْر qabla a(l)dh-dhur.

184

AL-QUDS AL-ARABI

يومية ـ سياسية ـ مستقلة

Headline of the Arabic newspaper "al-Quds al-Arabi", an independent pan-Arab daily newspaper published in London since 1989.

Arabic Jerusalem	al-quds al-ʿarabiyy	القُدس العَرَبيّ	ا ل قُ ذْ س ا ل عَ رَ ب يّ	القُدْس العَرَبيّ

Another commonly used root word from which many words are derived is q-r-a' قرأ "to read".

to read	qara'a	قَرَأ	قَ رَ أ	قَرَأ
reading	qirā'ah	قِرآءة	قِ ر آ ءَ ة	قِرآءة
reciter, reader	qārī'	قارِئ	ق ا رِ ئ	قارِئ
the Noble Qur'an (lit. the recital)	al-qur'ān al-karīm	القُرآن الكَريم	ا ل قُ ر آ ن ا ل ك رَ ي م	القُرآن الكَريم
Let's read!	hayyā naqra'	هَيَّا نَقْرَأ	هَ يّ ا نَ قْ رَ أ	هَيَّا نَقْرَأ

So far we learned that the Arabic for "west" is غَرْب. Look at the compass that follows and try to learn all four directions.

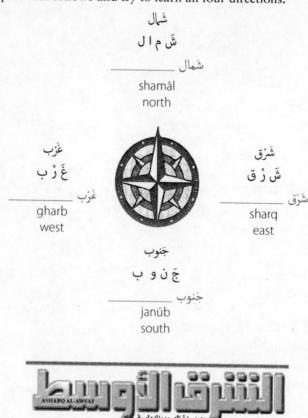

شَمال

شَ م ا ل

شمال
shamāl
north

غَرْب

غَ زْ ب

غَرْب
gharb
west

شَرْق

شَ رْ ق

شَرْق
sharq
east

جَنوب

جَ ن و ب

جَنوب
janūb
south

الشَّرْقُ الأوْسَط is a well-known Arabic international newspaper initially founded in London in 1978 and distributed worldwide.

الشَّرْقُ الأوْسَط

ال شَّ رْ قُ ال أ وْ سَ ط

الشَّرْقُ الأوْسَط
a(l)sh-sharq al-'awsaṭ
Middle East

Arabic names

The following names are common to both genders. For female names, you only need to add the feminine suffix ة/ـة. Note that most names in Arabic have actual meanings and can be adjectives you can use either in writing or speaking.

safe	'amīn/ah	أمين/ة	أ م ي ن /ة	أمين/ة
prince/princess	'amīr/ah	أمير/ة	أ م ي ر /ة	أمير/ة
beautiful	jamīl/ah	جَميل/ة	ج م ي ل /ة	جَميل/ة
happy, content	saʿīd/ah	سَعيد/ة	س ع ي د /ة	سَعيد/ة

minute	daqīqah	دَقيقَة	دَقيقَة	دَقيقَة
minutes	daqāʾiq	دَقائِق	دَ ق ا ئ ق	دَقائِق
embassy	sifārah	سِفارة	سِ ف ا ر ة	سِفارة
open	maftūh	مَفتوح	مَ ف ت و ح	مَفتوح
closed	maqfūl	مَقفول	مَ ق ف و ل	مَقفول
market (souk)	sūq	سوق	س و ق	سوق
train	qiṯār	قِطار	ق ط ا ر	قِطار
stop	qif	قِف	ق ف	قِف

قِف is a road sign found commonly in the Arab world. In certain Arab countries, they are written both in Arabic and along with the word "STOP".

The word shown at the front of this ambulance is written back to front. Can you write it in the correct way?

فُنْدُق

فُ نْ دُ ق

فُنْدُق_____

funduq
hotel

What is the name of the hotel?

المَركَز الثَّقافِيّ الإسْبانِيّ

ال مَ ركَ ز ال ثَّ ق ا فِ يّ ال إ س ب ا نِ يّ

المَركَز الثَّقافِيّ الإسبانِي ـ

al-markaz a(l)th-thaqāfiyy al-'isbāniyy

Spanish Cultural Centre

Insight
You already speak Arabic!

Here are some more Arabic loanwards used in English:

zero, cipher	sifr	صِفْر	صِ ف ر	صِفْر
sofa	suffah	صُفَّة	صُ فَّ ة	صُفَّة
giraffe	zarāfah	زَرافَة	زَ ر ا فَ ة	زَرافَة
cotton	qutn	قُطْن	قُ طْ ن	قُطْن
coffee	qahwah	قَهْوَة	قَ هْ وَ ة	قَهْوَة
candy	al-qand	القَنْد	ا ل قَ نْ د	القَنْد

ARABIC QUOTATION حِكْمَة عَرَبِيَّة

$$\text{الْجَارُ قَبْلَ الدَّارِ وَالرَّفِيقُ قَبْلَ الطَّرِيق}$$

al-jaar qabla a(l)-ddar wa a(l)-rrafiiq qabla a(l)-ttariiq

Seek the neighbour before the house and the companion before the journey

Arabic proverb

Circle the letters ف ق wherever you see them in the quoteation
Do you recognize any familiar words in the quotation that you
have learned so far?

SUMMARY TABLE

The following table is a summary of what you need to know about
the letters ف ق.

Pronunciation	Joined up	Final	Medial	Initial	Isolated	Name
/f/ in five	ففف	ـف	ـفـ	فـ	ف	فاءٌ Fā'
/q/	ققق	ـق	ـقـ	قـ	ق	قافٌ Qāf

Test yourself

Exercise 1
Read out loud and combine the letters to form words.

س و ق	أ ضْ فَ ر أَصْفَر صِ فْ ر
قِ فْ	قَ ه ْ وَ ة بُ رْ تُ قَ ا ل

Exercise 2
Read out loud and write the unjoined forms of the letters that make up the following words.

هاتف   فِلَسْطين   فِ لَ سْ ط ي ن   أَزْرَق

فُنْدُق   سِفارة   إِسْعاف

Exercise 3
Transliterate the words in Exercises 1 and 2 into roman script.

Exercise 4
Place the words in Exercises 1 and 2 into the right category.

Food	Countries	Colours	Public signs	Numbers

Exercise 5
Match the following public signs with their correct Arabic text.

مَفْتوح   Closed

مَقْفول   Open

Exercise 6
What is the English equivalent of the following Arabic loanwords?

صِفْر   قُطْن   زَرافَة   صُفَّة   قَمَرَة

Exercise 7
Read the following expressions and translate into English.

المَرْكَز الثَّقافِيّ   القُرآن الكَريم   الشَّرْقُ الأَوْسَط

Exercise 8

What is the message illustrated in this warning advert? (جميعا ضد = we are all against)

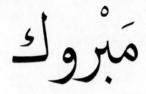

مَبْروك

mabruuk

Congratulations!

You have now reached the end of all the Arabic letters including the vowels and pronunciation symbols. By now, if you have studied all the units gradually and completed all the tests, you should be able to read and write virtually any Arabic script that you come across.

Unit 11

....

Arabic transcription

This unit deals with how foreign words are transcribed in the
Arabic script. You will be introduced to supplementary letters used
to adapt certain unfamiliar sounds that do not exist in Arabic e.g.
v in Volvo, p in pope, g in game, etc.

Arabic has, like many other languages, a capacity to absorb and
accommodate borrowings from other languages. The reverse is
also true and Arabic has contributed much to other languages.
Originally, the Arabic alphabet was first used to document in
writing the aurally memorized Qur'an. With the spread of Islam
across the world, its chief vehicle of language, Arabic, spread to
other cultures and countries and came into direct contact with their
languages, especially Spanish, Persian, Pashto, Malay, Swahili,
Urdu, Panjabi, Kashmiri, Kurdish, Turkish, Indonesian, and, more
recently, languages such as English, French and many more.

In order for Arabic to accommodate new and foreign sounds of
the languages in which it came into contact, additional letters and
symbols had to be introduced into the original Arabic alphabet (see
table at the beginning of this book).

Arabic transcription is a way of writing foreign words (originally
Latin script or any other) using the Arabic script. Nowadays it
is commonly seen in advertising language. Foreign visitors to the
Arab world will quickly notice a remarkable and colourful range of
bilingual commercial signs for foreign corporations in Arabic, such
as McDonald's, Coca-Cola, KFC, etc.

These signs are transcribed exactly as they are pronounced by Arabic speakers instead of how they are spelt in their original language.

Foreign word	Arabic spelling
McDonald's	Mākdonāldz
Mr. Jones	Mister Jūwnz
pizza	pītzā
taxi	tāksī

In my experience, it is always entertaining to watch students enjoy the moment and the delight of being able to decode a well-known foreign name written in Arabic, after struggling to read it for some time!

Normally, there are no set standard rules for Arabic transcription; however, as a rule of thumb remember the following:

1 When it comes to commercial signs, don't always assume they are Arabic words! Most of them are simply transcribed foreign names such as cafeteria, supermarket, etc.
2 Some signs that can be easily translated into proper Arabic are deliberately written in their original language, e.g. café, sweet, home, Topshop, wicked!, etc.
3 In most signs, you will notice some recognisable visual clues that will help you read the sign quickly, e.g. company logo, script style, brand colours, etc.
4 Short vowels are left out in advertising signs and when writing foreign words. However, the long vowels ا و ي are used instead.

Translation	Example	Arabic vowels	Foreign vowel
plaza	بلازا	ا	a
Pepsi	بيبسي	ي	i, e
Coca-Cola	كوكاكولا	و	o, u

5 Try to read out the words fully loud and not letter by letter. They are usually pronounced a little differently than in their original language.

6 Do not give up! Keep trying to sound out the words in the sign several times with different pronunciations. You will be surprised to find out that you are likely to know the word already.

7 Sometimes, in cases in which supplementary letters may not be used, foreign words and sounds may be Arabized using the closest Arabic letters. For example, "Seven-Up" can be written either:

$$\text{سفن أب} \quad \text{or} \quad \text{سڤن أپ}$$

8 To be able to read foreign words in Arabic correctly and promptly, familiarize yourself with the following supplementary letters and their approximate equivalent in Arabic alphabetical letters.

Foreign word	Example in Arabic	Arabic letters	Supplementary letters	Foreign sound
super	سوبر	ب	پ	p in pope
garage	كراج	ك / ج	گ / ڭ	g in game
chair	تشير	تش	چ	ch in check
volvo	فولفو	ف	ڤ	v in volvo
azure	أزور	ز	ژ	z in zoo

These supplementary letters are also primarily used in Persian, Urdu, and Kurdish.

A trilingual sign displaying transcribed foreign words in Arabic

Images of signs with foreign words transcribed in Arabic are widely available online and increasingly shared freely by travelers and holiday makers via photo-sharing sites like Flickr and Picasa or photo blogs.

Commercial signs and other realia materials containing foreign names are excellent visual learning resources for consolidating your reading skills of the Arabic script.

For more practice in reading different scripts, go to the Visual Arabic Library at v-Arabic.com/vra.

Test yourself

The following sign show foreign words transcribed in Arabic. Can you recognize them?

Read out loud and write their equivalent in the space provided.

The foreign words have been blanked out in some signs.

_____   _____

_____

_____

_____

ألــوان • جمــــال • تـألـق

Hajj & Umrah Ltd

Packages to Arab & Islamic World

ساهسونج

The following sign is the name of a restaurant in Morocco. The name is that of a famous tree commonly referred to as "the tree of life".

أركانة

طاكسيات

Unit **12**

Arabic handwriting

Arabic handwriting is a simplified version of the printed script.
This unit looks at the style of handwriting compared to print style
with real-life samples to help you improve your reading skills even
further, especially of the handwritten script.

The most adopted script for daily handwriting is known as Ruqᶜah
(الرُّقْعَة), i.e. small sheet, which is an easy script to learn and read.
Here is an example of Ruqᶜah.

Print style

Ruqᶜah style

أهلاً وسهلاً ومرحباً   أهلاً وسهلاً ومرحباً

Generally speaking, the difference between handwritten and
printed style is not as major as in Latin script. Unlike the latter,
both forms in Arabic are cursive in writing. The Ruqᶜah style is
distinguished by its clipped letters with straight lines and small
curves.

Let us examine the main and subtle differences between the two
styles:

1 The two dots of the Arabic letters ي ق ت are sometimes
   handwritten like a straight dash "-" above or below the dotted
   letters. Do not confuse this dash with the diagonal stroke of

Fatha (◌َ). Here are the three dotted letters written in the four positions:

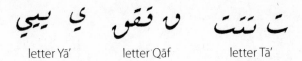

letter Yā'   letter Qāf   letter Tā'

2 The three dots of ش and ث are handwritten as a cap or French circumflex "^".

letter Shīn   letter Tā'

3 Certain letters such as ن ض ق are handwritten without their dots and all end with a hook when written in the final form.

4 The most obvious difference between print and handwritten style is seen in the final and isolated positions of the letters ض ق ن. The table that follows highlights the differences between individual letters in isolated, initial, medial and final forms.

Handwriting	Print	Name
ع حـحـع	ح ححح	Ḥā'
This also applies to the other similar shaped letters of the same letter group, i.e. ج خ		
سـ سـسس	س سسس	Sīn
سـ شـشـش	ش ششش	Shīn
The three hooks of س and ش are usually handwritten as a straight line in all positions		

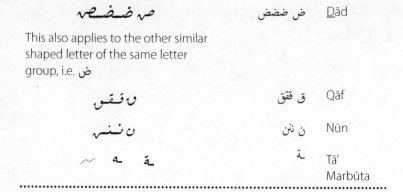

صو ضضصو	ض ضضض	Ḍād

This also applies to the other similar
shaped letter of the same letter
group, i.e. ض

ونقو	ق ققق	Qāf
ن ننس	ن ننن	Nūn
ح ـه ـة	ـة	Tā' Marbūta

With the wide spread of web-based communication tools (e.g. email, and instant messaging and computer-processed text, it is safe to say that throughout your learning of Arabic, you will encounter the Arabic script more frequently in printed than in handwritten style.

However, handwriting (especially the Ruqᶜah style) has not lost its popularity in the Arab world and it is still used for handwriting documents (e.g. scribbled notes, letters, announcements, etc.) as well as for marketing and advertisement (e.g. commercial signboards, road signs, book titles, etc.).

Remember, with continuous practice and repeated exposure to handwritten script style, you will learn to recognize it in no time.

Unit 13

Arabic calligraphy and script styles

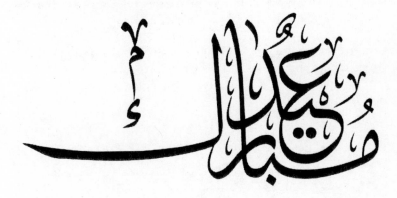

عيد مبارك

Happy Eid (i.e. festival)

You have now learned the whole Arabic script both in print and handwriting styles. This unit will introduce you to the visual beauty of the written Arabic script using a variety of calligraphic styles and script variants.

Unlike Roman languages, Arabic calligraphy has not fallen out of use and it is considered as a bridge between the literary heritage of the Arabic language and the religion of Islam. As a result, Arabic calligraphy is also widely referred to as Islamic calligraphy and more eloquently as 'the art of the pen' (فن القلم).

Arabic calligraphy, alongside Islamic geometrical designs, are commonly used to decorate mosques, architectural buildings, furniture, pottery, manuscripts and greeting cards, as well as to write down Qur'anic verses, poetry and wise quotes in spectacular composition and astonishing visual beauty.

Calligraphers, with their commitment to precision, elegance and artistic talents are regarded in high esteem and their tools (e.g. reed pen or calamus) are praised as the source of knowledge.

The cursive nature of the script allows Arabic to be written in a variety of spectacular works of art. In fact, there are over 100 varieties of Arabic calligraphy, including the major six script styles: Thuluth, Diwani, Kufic, Naskh, Ruq'ah, and Ruq'a.

To introduce you to the different calligraphic writings and script styles, we are going to use a famous and widely memorized Qur'anic phrase which occurs at the beginning of each chapter in the Qur'an[1]:

In the name of Allah the Most Merciful the Most compassionate

THULUTH (خَطّ الثُلُث)

Thuluth is a large and elegant cursive script with an ornamental writing style, famously used since the medieval times to write Qur'anic verses. It is commonly seen in mosque decorations, especially in Turkey (the home of Arabic calligraphy masters) and around the Arab/Muslim world.

---

[1] With the exception of the 9th chapter in the Qur'an.

DIWANI (الخطّ الدّيواني)

Diwani is a highly cursive style. It was labeled Diwani due to its exclusive use in the Ottoman diwan (i.e. royal court). It was used for writing all royal decrees, endowments and resolutions.

KUFIC (الخطّ الكوفي)

Kufic is the oldest calligraphic form of Arabic scripts. Its name is derived from the city of Kufa كوفة in Iraq. Kufic was the script in which the first copies of the Qur'an were written.

SQUARE KUFIC (الخَطّ الكوفي المُرَبَّع)

Square Kufic is another form of Kufic style easily distinguished by its squared lines and angles. Nowadays, this style is frequently used by calligraphers and typographers to design institution logos and short Qura'nic chapters. Both Kufic and square Kufic are written without vowels.

NASKH (خَطّ النَّسْخ)

Naskh meaning 'to copy' is a well-known style most commonly favoured for printing Arabic. Its beauty lies in the combination between traditional typography and fine calligraphic precision. It was derived from Thuluth with adaptations that simplified the script resulting in a smaller size and more elegant style.

RIQ^cA (خَطّ الرّقْعَة)

Riq^ca meaning 'small sheet' is used mostly for daily handwriting. It is an easy script to learn and read and is characterized by its clipped letters with straight lines and small curves.

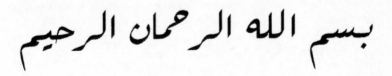

NASTA^cLĪQ (نَسْتَعْليق)

Nasta^clīq is a style used in writing the Perso-Arabic script, and a predominant style in Persian calligraphy. It has also been adopted in writing Dari, Uzbek, Turkmen (commonly spoken in Afghanistan) and Panjabi, Urdu and Kashmiri (in Pakistan).

Test yourself

Exercise 1
I am sure by now you have noticed that the cover of this book features the calligraphic illustration below. First, read the expression in print style then try to trace it in the calligraphic writing.

Hint: the expression reads from top to bottom.

Can you identify what type of calligraphy style it is written with?

إنَّ الله يُحِبّ إذا عَمِلَ أَحَدُكُم عَمَلاً أَنْ يُتقِنَهُ

*Certainly, Allah loves for one of you when performing
a deed to perform it with perfection*

Muhammad (the prophet)

Exercise 2
Can you recognize which country this flag or map represents?

Do you remember the meaning of the phrase written in the flag?
What type of calligraphy is it?

Exercise 3
Read and write the following phrases.

Do you remember their meanings?

Insight: Logos

Nowadays, Arabic calligraphy is widely used in designing logos, names of institutions, and tourist merchandise such as t-shirts.

The logo of Aljazeera TV station, a well-known international news network based in Qatar. The Arabic word Al-Jazeera literally means, 'The Island'.

Centre for the
Advanced
Study of the
Arab
World

The logo of CASAW (Centre for the Advanced Study of the Arab World) – a UK-based academic institution – written in square Kufic style.

Unit 14

Arabic ligatures and letter combinations

This unit demonstrates some of the common letter combinations used in Arabic writing, usually referred to as *ligatures*.

Arabic ligatures are special combinations of certain letters adopted by calligraphers who usually combine two or more letters in one unit in a continuous cursive stroke without lifting the pen, resulting in a ligature.

Besides using ligatures for aesthetic purposes, they are also used for preserving space and increasing writing speed.

A handwritten Arabic sentence written in ligatured combinations

الحج المبرور

/al-hajj al-mabrūr/

Accepted Hajj (pilgrimage)

In addition to handwritten calligraphy, ligatures are also being used in print or computer-based typesetting.

Ligatures appear in slightly different shapes than the normal handwritten ones you saw earlier in this book and are typically known to cause some confusion to Arabic learners at first sight. One of the ways to familiarize yourself with these combinations is through extensive reading and frequent exposure.

The following table contains some of the common ligatures.

Non-ligatured script	ligatures	letter combinations		
				←
بج / بحـ	جـ / بحـ	حٌ *	+	ب ت ث ي ن
بم / بمـ	بم / بمـ	م		
لم / لمـ	لم / لمـ	م		ل
لح / لحـ	لح / لحـ	حٌ *	+	
لي	لي	ي		
جح / جحـ	جح / جحـ	حٌ *	+	ج ح خ
حه	حه	ه		
سح / سحـ	سح / سحـ	حٌ *	+	س
سم / سمـ	سم / سمـ	م		
عم / عمـ	عم / عمـ	م	+	ع
مم / ممـ	مم / ممـ	م	+	م
مي	مي	ي		
في	في	ي	+	ف
هم / همـ	هم / همـ	م	+	ه
يج / يجـ	يج / يجـ	حٌ *	+	ي
يم / يمـ	يم / يمـ	م		

* Including all the letters of the letter group no. 6 (i.e. ج ح خ).

There are two commonly known ligatures in Arabic writing:

1 Due to its frequent use in Arabic, one notable ligatured word to highlight is the word Allah (i.e. God) usually written in calligraphy and now in printed or computerized typesetting. Using any text-processing software such as MS Word, if you type the letters *Alif, Lām, Lām and Hā'*, you will get this unique ligatured word along with the accompanying automated vowel signs (*shaddah* and *dagger Alif*):

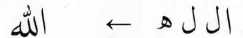

2 The second most frequently used ligatured word in calligraphy and print is the word ﻻ (i.e. no), which – as explained in Unit 1 can appear in a variety of script styles.

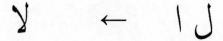

Unit 15

....

Arabic root word system

A well-connected language!
Among the fascinating aspects of Arabic is its root word system
and how the vocabulary is remarkably and logically connected,
both in root words and meaning.

Once you are familiar with how the roots work you will be able to
unleash the meaning of a huge body of vocabulary and untangle
many unknown words, especially if studied in context. In fact,
you can easily start guessing the meaning of numerous derivative
words and patterns (some roots have as many as 40 derivatives) of
one single root word, and you may even be able to produce words
correctly from an established set of patterns.

Verbs are formed from a tri-consonantal root or radical combined
with patterns that consist of prefixes and suffixes. For each root,
one can derive up to 15 verb forms. These forms are referred to
by Western grammarians as "form I-X". From these forms, there
are many derivative participles and verbal nouns that are the main
source of constructing vocabulary in Arabic.

To illustrate this concept, let us look at the following example:

In English, from the verb *read*, we may derive:

    read (past tense)
    reading
    reader

readership
read-out
read-in
etc.

In Arabic, from the tri-consonanatal root k-t-b we can derive at
least 15 words. All these words share the three consonants k-t-b
(ك ت ب) and all connected to the meaning of writing.

English	Transliteration			Arabic
to write	kataba	كَتَب	كَ تَ بَ	كَتَبَ
books	kutub	كتُب	كُ تُ ب	كُتُب
to force someone to write	kattaba	كَتَّب	كَ تَّ ب	كَتَّب
book	kitāb	كِتاب	كِ ت ا ب	كِتاب
writing	kitābah	كِتابَة	كِ ت ا ب ة	كِتابَة
to correspond	kātaba	كائَب	كـ ا تَ بَ	كاتَبَ
writer (m.f.)	kātib/ah	كاتِب /ة	كـ ا تِ ب/ة	كاتِب/ة
writers	kuttāb	كتّاب	كُ تَّ ا ب	كُتّاب
office, desk	maktab	مَكتَب	مَ كـ تَ ب	مَكتَب
bookshop, library	maktabah	مَكتَبَة	مَ كـ تَ بَ ة	مَكتَبَة
correspondence	mukātabah	مُكائَبَة	مُ كـ ا تَ بَ ة	مُكاتَبَة
written	maktūb	مَكتوب	مَ كـ تَ و ب	مَكتوب

Study the following diagram.

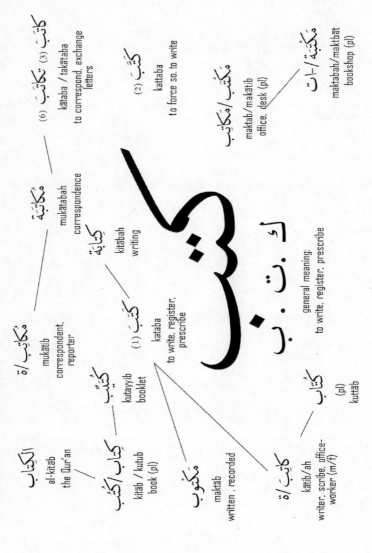

ا ل ك ت ا ب
al-kitāb
the Qur'an

كِتَاب / كُتُب
kitāb / kutub
book (pl)

مَكْتُوب
maktab
written , recorded

كَاتِب / ة
kātib/ah
writer, scribe, office-
worker (m/f)

كُتَّاب
(pl)
kuttāb

كُتَيِّب
kutayyib
booklet

مُكَاتِب / ة
mukātib
correspondent,
reporter

(1) كَتَبَ
kataba
to write, register,
prescribe

كِتَابَة
kitābah
writing

مُكَاتَبَة
mukātabah
correspondence

ك ت ب
general meaning:
to write, register, prescribe

(6) كَاتَبَ تَكَاتَبَ (3)
kataba / takātaba
to correspond, exchange
letters

(2) كَتَّبَ
kattaba
to force so. to write

مَكْتَب / مَكَاتِب
maktab/makātib
office, desk (pl)

مَكْتَبَة / ات-
maktabah/maktabāt
bookshop (pl)

216

Appendices

Vocabulary

مفردات الألوان COLOURS

لون. ج ألوان	lawn / 'alwān	colour(s)
أَبْيَض / بَيْضاء	'abyad / baydā'	white
أَحْمَر / حَمْراء	'ahmar / hamrā'	red
أَخْضَر / خَضْراء	'akhdar / khadrā'	green
أَزْرَق / زَرْقاء	'azraq / zarqā'	blue
أَسْوَد / سَوْداء	aswad / sawdā'	black
أَصْفَر / صَفْراء	asfar / safrā'	yellow
بَنَفْسَجِيّ / ة أو أُرْجُوانِيّ / ة	'urjuwāni / banafsajī	purple
بُرْتُقالِيّ / ة	burtuqāliyy	orange
بُنِّيّ / ة	bunniyy	brown
رَمادِيّ / ة	ramādiyy	gray
وَرْدِي / ة	wardiyy	pink
غامِق / داكِن	ghāmiq/dākin	dark (colour)
فاتِح	fātih	light (colour)

DAYS OF THE WEEK أيام الأسبوع

يَوْمُ الإِثْنَين	yawm al-'ithnayn	Monday
يَوْمُ الثُّلاثاء	yawm a(l)th-thulathā'	Tuesday
يَوْمُ الأَرْبِعاء	yawm al-'arbiᶜā'	Wednesday
يَوْمُ الخَمِيس	yawm al-khamīs	Thursday
يَوْمُ الجُمْعَة	yawm al-jumuᶜa	Friday
يَوْمُ السَّبْت	yawm a(l)s-sabt	Saturday
يَوْمُ الأَحَد	yawm al-'aḥad	Sunday

ARABIC GREGORIAN CALENDAR مفردات الوقت: التقويم الميلادي

كانون الثّاني	kānūn-a(l)th-thānī	يَناير	yanāyir	January
شُباط	shubbāṭ	فَبْرايِر	fabryāyir	February
آذار	'ādhār	مارِس	mārs	March
نيسان	nīsān	أَبْريل	'aprīl	April
أيار	'ayār	مايُو	māyū	May
حزيران	ḥazīrān	يُونيُو	yūnyū	June
تموز	tammūz	يُوليُو	yūlū	July
آب	'āb	أَغْسْطُس	'aghusṭus	August
أيْلول	'aylūl	سَبْتَمْبر	sabtambar	September
تِشرينُ الأوّل	tishrīn al-'awwal	أُكْتُوبَر	'uktūbar	October
تِشرينُ الثّاني	tishrīn a(t)th-thānī	نُوفَمْبر	nūvambar	November
كانونُ الأوّل	kānūn al-'awwal	دِيسَمْبر	dīsambar	December

FAMILY MEMBERS

أُسْرَة	'usrah	family
أَب / وَالِد	'ab / wālid	father
أُم / وَالِدَة	'umm / wālida	mother
أَخ	'akh	brother
أُخْت	'ukht	sister
اِبْن	'ibn	son
اِبْنَة / بِنْت	'ibna / bint	daughter
عَمّ	ᶜamm	paternal uncle
عَمَّة	ᶜammah	paternal aunt
خَال	khāl	maternal uncle
خَالَة	khālah	maternal aunt
اِبْن عَمّ	'ibn ᶜamm	paternal cousin
اِبْن عَمَّة	'ibn ᶜamma	paternal cousin

PUBLIC SIGNS AND NOTICES

Arabic	Pronunciation	English
مَطار	maṯār	airport
مَقْهى	maqhā	café
مَتْجَر	matjar	shop
دُكَّان	dukkān	grocery
فُنْدُق	funduq	hotel
مُسْتَشْفى	mustashfā	hospital
مَكْتَبَة	maktabah	library, bookshop
حَلَّاق	ḥallāq	barber

مَتْحَف	mathaf	museum
مَطْعَم	mat‘am	restaurant
مَدْرَسَة	madrasah	school
جامِعَة	jāmi‘ah	university
مَمْنوع التَّدْخين	mamnū‘ a(l)t-tadkhīn	smoking forbidden
مَمْنوع الدُّخول	mamnū‘ a(l)d-dukhūl	no entry
ممنوع الوقوف	mamnū‘ al-wuqūf	no stopping/parking
مَمْنوع التَّصْوير	mamnū‘ a(l)ttaṣwīr	no photography
الرَّجاء عَدَم	a(l)r-rajā’ ‘adam	please do not
خُروج	khurūj	exit
دُخول	dukhūl	entry
وُصول	wuṣūl	arrival
خَطَر	khaṭar	danger
مَفْتوح	maftūh	open
مُغْلَق	mughlaq	closed
اِدْفَع	’idfa‘	push
اِسْحَب	’ishab	pull
دَوْرَة المِياه	dawrat al-miyāh	toilet, WC
شُرْطَة	shurṭah	police
سوق	sūq	market
خاصّ	khāṣ	private
قِفْ	qif	stop
تاكْسيات	tāksiyāt	taxis
رِجال	rijāl	men
سَيِّدات	sayyidāt	ladies
ساخِن	sākhin	hot
بارِد	bārid	cold

Numbers

CARDINAL NUMBERS

Hindu numbers	Standard Arabic numbers	Pronunciation	Handwriting practice	Arabic name (print form)
٠	0	ṣifr	صِفْرٌ	صِفْر
١	1	wāḥid	واحِدٌ	واحِد
٢	2	'ithnān	إثْنانِ	إثْنانِ
٣	3	thalātha	ثَلاثَةٌ	ثَلاثَة
٤	4	'arbaᶜah	أَرْبَعَةٌ	أَرْبَعَة
٥	5	khamsah	خَمْسَةٌ	خَمْسَة
٦	6	sittah	سِتَّةٌ	سِتَّة
٧	7	sabᶜah	سَبْعَةٌ	سَبْعَة
٨	8	thamāniyah	ثَمانِيَةٌ	ثَمانِية
٩	9	tisᶜah	تِسْعَةٌ	تِسْعَة
١٠	10	ᶜasharah	عَشَرَةٌ	عَشَرَة
١١	11	'aḥada ᶜashar	أحَدَ عَشَر	أَحَدَ عَشَر
١٢	12	'ithnā ᶜashar	إثْنا عَشَر	إثْنا عَشَر
١٣	13	thalāthat ᶜashar	ثَلاثَةَ عَشَر	ثَلاثَةَ عَشَر
١٤	14	'arbaᶜata ᶜashar	أرْبَعَةَ عَشَر	أرْبَعَةَ عَشَر
١٥	15	khamsata ᶜashar	خَمْسَةَ عَشَر	خَمْسَةَ عَشَر

١٦	16	sittata ᶜashar	سِتَّةَ عَشَر	سِتَّةَ عَشَر
١٧	17	sabᶜata ᶜashar	سَبْعَةَ عَشَر	سَبْعَةَ عَشَر
١٨	18	thamāniyata ᶜashar	ثَمانِيَةَ عَشَر	ثَمَانِيَةَ عَشَر
١٩	19	tisᶜata ᶜashar	تِسْعَةَ عَشَر	تِسْعَةَ عَشَر
٢٠	20	ᶜishrūn	عِشْرُون	عِشْرُون
٣٠	30	thalāthūn	ثَلاثُون	ثَلاثُون
٤٠	40	'arbaᶜūn	أرْبَعُون	أَرْبَعُون
٥٠	50	khamsūn	خَمْسُون	خَمْسُون
٦٠	60	sittūn	سِتُّون	سِتُّون
٧٠	70	sabᶜūn	سَبْعُون	سَبْعُون
٨٠	80	thamānūn	ثَمانون	ثَمَانون
٩٠	90	tisᶜūn	تِسْعون	تِسْعون
١٠٠	100	mi'ah	مائة	مائة
٢٠٠	200	mi'atān	مائَتانِ	مائَتانِ
١٠٠٠	1000	'alf	ألف	ألْف
٢٠٠٠	2000	'alfān	ألْفانِ	ألْفانِ
١٠,٠٠٠	10,000	ᶜashrat 'alāf	عَشَرَةُ آلافٍ	عَشَرَةُ آلافٍ
١٠٠,٠٠٠	100,000	mi'at 'alf	مائَةُ ألْفٍ	مائَةُ ألْفٍ
١,٠٠٠,٠٠٠	1,000,000	malyūn	مَلْيُون	مَلْيُون
٢,٠٠٠,٠٠٠	2,000,000	malyūnān	مَلْيُونانِ	مَلْيُونانِ
١٠٠٠,٠٠٠,٠٠٠	1,000,000,000	balyūn	بَلْيُون	بَلْيُون

Modern-day keypad ATMs, car plate numbers, etc. usually display Western Arabic/European numerals alongside Eastern Arabic–Hindi numerals.

Arabic numbers are mostly used in Western Arabic countries like in this gigantic advert in Morocco and the speed sign. Hindi numbers are rarely used in these countries.

ORDINAL NUMBERS

1st	al-'awwal / al-'ūlā	الأوّل / الأولى	الأوّل/ الأولى
2nd	a(l)-ththānī /-yah	الثَّاني/ة	الثَّاني/ة
3rd	a(l)-ththālith /-ah	الثَّالِث/ة	الثَّالِث/ة
4th	a(l)-rrābiᶜ /-ah	الرَّابِع /ة	الرَّابِع/ة
5th	al-khāmis /-ah	الخامِس /ة	الخامِس/ة
6th	a(l)-ssādis /-ah	السَّادِس /ة	السَّادِس/ة
7th	a(l)-ssabiᶜ /ah	السَّابِع /ة	السَّابِع/ة
8th	a(l)-ththāmin /-ah	الثَّامِن /ة	الثَّامِن/ة
9th	a(l)-ttāsiᶜ /-ah	التَّاسِع /ة	التَّاسِع/ة
10th	al-ᶜāshir /-ah	العاشِر /ة	العاشِر/ة
11th	al-ḥādī ᶜashar	الحادي /ة عشر	الحادي/ة عشر
12th	a(l)th-thāni ᶜashar	الثَّاني /ة عَشر	الثَّاني/ة عَشر
13th	a(l)th-thālith ᶜashar	الثَّالَث /ة عشر	الثَّالَث/ة عشر
14th	a(l)r-rābiᶜ ᶜashar	الرَّابِع /ة عشر	الرَّابِع/ة عشر
15th	al-khāmis ᶜashar	الخامِس /ة عشر	الخامِس/ة عشر
16th	a(l)s-sādis ᶜashar	السَّادِس /ة عشر	السَّادِس/ة عشر
17th	a(l)s-sabiᶜ ᶜashar	السَّابِع /ة عشر	السَّابِع/ة عشر
18th	a(l)th-thāmin ᶜashar	الثَّامِن /ة عشر	الثَّامِن/ة عشر
19th	a(l)t-tāsiᶜᶜashar	التَّاسِع /ة عشر	التَّاسِع/ة عشر
20th	al-ᶜishrūn	العِشْرون	العِشْرون

21st	al-ḥādī wal-ᶜishrūn	الحادي والعِشْرون	الحادي والعِشْرون
22nd	a(l)th-thānī wal-ᶜishrūn	الثَّاني /ة وَالعِشْرون	الثَّاني/ة وَالعِشْرون
30th	ath-thalāthūn	الثَّلاثون	الثَّلاثون
40th	al-'arbaᶜūn	الأَرْبَعون	الأَرْبَعون
50th	al-khamsūn	الخَمْسون	الخَمْسون
60th	a(l)s-sittūn	السِّتّون	السِّتّون
70th	a(l)s-sabᶜūn	السَّبْعون	السَّبْعون
80th	a(l)th-thamānūn	الثَّمانون	الثَّمانون
90th	a(l)t-tisᶜūn	التِسعون	التِسعون
100th	al-miʾah	المِئَة / المِائَة	المِئَّة / المائَّة

Arabic alphabet as numerals

The use of alphabetical letters to represent numbers in Arabic is similar to numbering paragraphs in English using the letters (a, b, c, etc.). This numeral system is called Abjab numerals or letters (الحروف الأبجدية). The order of the letters are different from the alphabet table you learned so far (ا ب ت ث ج ح خ ...).

The numeral order of the alphabet is that of the old Semitic alphabet, so Alif is 1, Baa' is 2, Jiim is 3, and so on until ten which is followed by 20, 30, etc. and then 100, 200, 300, etc.

To memorize this order, Arabs usually poetry lines (which, in this case, is meaningless) as a memory technique. The line goes like:

أَبَجَد هَوَّز حُطِّي كَلَمَن   سَعَفَص قُرِشَت ثُخَّذ ضَظَغ

This numbering system is not commonly used; however, you might notice in train stations that platforms 1, 2, 3, etc. are numbered alphabetically as ا ب ج ...

ي	ط	ح	ز	و	ه	د	ج	ب	أ
10	9	8	7	6	5	4	3	2	1

ع	س	ص	ف	ن	م	ل	ك
90	80	70	60	50	40	30	20

ض	ذ	خ	ث	ت	ش	ر	ق	غ	ظ
1000	900	800	700	600	500	400	300	200	100

Arabic loanwords in English

Arabic word	Pronunciation	Meaning
الكُحول	al-kuhūl	alcohol
الجَبر	al-jabr	algebra (meaning restoring or combination)
الخَوارِزمي	al-khawārizmī	algorithm (name of the mathematician who invented Algebra)
دارُ الصِّناعَة	dār a(l)s-sinā‘a	arsenal (meaning house of industry)
أطلَس	’atlas	atlas
البادِنجان	al-bādhinjān	aubergine
العَوارِيَّة	al-‘awāriyya	average
القَمَرَة	al-qamarah	camera (meaning 'dark room' translated as *camera obscura*)
القَنْد	al-qand	candy (meaning 'liquid of sugar cane')
الشّاه مات	a(l)sh-shāh māt	checkmate (meaning 'the king died')
الصكّ	a(l)s-saq	cheque

قَهْوَة	qahwa	coffee
الغيتَارَة	al-guītāra	guitar
الزَّهْر	a(l)z-zahr	hazard
مَخَازِن	makhāzin	magazine (meaning storehouse)
مَطْرَح	maṭrah	mattress
راحَة	rāḥa	racket (meaning palm of the hand)
صُداع	sodāᶜ	soda, sodium (meaning headache)
صُفَّة	ṣuffa	sofa
سُكَّر	sukkar	sugar
شَراب	sharāb	syrup (meaning drink)
صِفْر	ṣifr	zero, cipher

Common Arabic names and terms

COMMON ARABIC NAMES

Names for men		Names for women	
أبو	'abū + name of first child	أم	'umm + name of first child
عَبْدُ الله	ᶜabdullah	عائِشَة	ᶜā'ishah
عَبْدُ الرحْمان	ᶜabdu-rrahmān	فَريدَة	farīdah
مُحَمَّد	muhammad	سارَة	sārah
مَحْمود	mahmūd	فاطِمَة	fāṭimah
أسامَة	'usāmah	حَنان	ḥanān

أَحْمَد	'ahmad	خَديجَة	khadījah
عَلي	ʿalī	ريم	rīm
عيسى	ʿīsā	زَيْنَب	zaynab
حَسَن	ḥasan	سَعيدة	saʿīdah
حُسَين	ḥusayn	سُعاد	suʿād
إبْراهيم	'ibrāhīm	لَيْلى	laylā
جَعْفَر	jaʿfar	نَجيبَة	najībah
جَميل	jamīl	ياسْمين	yāsmīn
جَمال	jamāl		
خالِد	khālid		
گَمال	kamāla		
موسى	mūsā		
مُصْطَفى	muṣṭafā		
ناصِر	nāsir		
عُمَر	ʿumar		
سَليم	salīm		
سَمير	samīr		
سُلَيْمان	sulaimān		
ياسِر	yāsir		
طارِق	ṭāriq		
يوسُف	yūsuf		
يَحْيى	yahyā		

COMMONLY USED ISLAMIC TERMS

Arabic	Transliteration	English
الله	'allāh	God
السلام عليكم	a(l)s-salāmu ᶜalaikum	hello (lit. peace be upon you)
رب	rabb	lord
صيام	ṣiyām	fasting
الحمد الله	al-ḥamdu lillāh	thanks be to God
ما شاء الله	mā shā' allāh	
إن شاء الله	'in shā' allāh	if God wills
القرآن الكريم	al-qur'ān al-karīm	the noble Qur'an
حج	hajj	pilgrimage
مسلم/ة	muslim/ah	Muslim
الاسلام	al-'islām	Islam
نبي	nabiyy	prophet
رسول	rasūl	messenger
عيد الفطر	ᶜīd al-fitr	festival of…
عيد الأضحى	ᶜīd al-'aḍhā	festival of the sacrifice

Western letters in Arabic style

To give the English script – or any other Romance language for that matter – an Arabic or Eastern look, there has recently been an increasing use of a new type of writing commonly referred to as *pseudo-* or *faux-Arabic.*

Pseudo-Arabic is an attempt to compose Latin script by emulating (to a certain extent) the appearance of Arabic calligraphy script.

Although Arab speakers might find pseudo-Arabic puzzling and some would struggle to decipher it, it is mostly quite legible to speakers of Latin languages.

There is a variety of computer-based typesetting, which include upper and lower case Latin alphabets, numerals and punctuation marks.

"The Qur'an" written in pseudo-Arabic
Do you recognize any Arabic letters within the text?

Here is how the title of this book can appear in pseudo-Arabic.

Read and write

arabic script

Grammar

ONE-LETTER WORDS

Letter words are not written independently and are always attached to the following word and each one of them carries a specific meaning and grammatical function.

Be aware that when these one-letter particles are connected to the following word they might look as if it were one word. As you learn more vocabulary, you will become more familiar with connected words/phrases.

Bear in mind that:

- The Alif of (ال) is dropped when connected to ل e.g. لل = ال + ل.
- The second Lām of (لل) is either silent or sounded, depending on the letter type (sun or moon) e.g. للمدرسة = المدرسة + ل.

The following table contains is a list of commonly used one-word particles in Arabic.

Arabic letter word	Transliteration	Translation
و	wa	and
أ	'a	yes and no question initial interrogative particle that indicates a yes or no question usually precedes a noun or a pronoun, not a verb or an adjective. It is written together with the following word as a one-letter word
كَ	ka	as, like
سَ	sa	will
لِ	li	for, to
فَ	fa	thus, therefore

POSSESSIVE PRONOUNS (ATTACHED)

Translation	Pronunciation	Possessive pronoun	
my pen	ī	ي	
your pen (m.)	ka	كَ	
your pen (f.)	ki	كِ	
his pen	hu	ـه	
her pen	hā	ها	قلم +
our pen	nā	نا	
your pen (m. pl.)	kum	كُم	noun +
your pen (f. pl.)	kunna	كُن	
their pen (m. pl.)	hum	هُم	
their pen (f. pl.)	hunna	هُن	
their pen (dual, f. m.)	kumā	كُما	

OBJECT PRONOUNS (ATTACHED)

Translation	Pronunciation	Object pronoun
he taught me	ni	ني
he taught you (m.)	ka	كَ
he taught you (f.)	ki	كِ
he taught him	hu	هـ
he taught her	hā	ها
he taught us	nā	نا
he taught you (m. pl.)	kum	كُم
he taught you (f. pl.)	kunna	كُنّ
he taught them (m. pl.)	hum	هُم
I taught them (f. pl.)	hunna	هُنّ
he taught them (dual, f. m.)	kumā	كُما
he taught them (dual, f. m.)	humā	هُما

عَلَّمَ +

verb +

SUBJECT PRONOUNS (SEPARATE)

Translation	Pronunciation	Subject pronoun
I	'anā	أَنَا
you (m.)	'anta	أَنْتَ
you (f.)	'anti	أَنْتِ
he	huwa	هُوَ
she	hiya	هِيَ
you (dual)	'antumā	أَنْتُما
they (dual)	humā	هُمَأ
we (pl.)	nahnu	نَحْنُ
you (m. pl.)	'antum	أَنْتُمْ
you (f. pl.)	'antunna	أَنْتُنَّ
they (m. pl.)	hum	هُمْ
they (f. pl.)	hunna	هُنَّ

Key to the exercises

Arabic vowels and pronunciation symbols

Short vowels
da, du, di du, da, di da, du, di, di, da, du, darasa, durisa, darisa,
durasa, dirusa, darusa, dirasa

Long vowels
dā, dā, dā dā, dā, dā dā, dā, dā daaris, daarasa, darasaa, diraasa,
madaaris, duruus, madruus, darsii, madaaresii

Tanween
dan, din, dun dan, dun, din dan, din, dun darsan, darsun, darsin,
madrasatan, madrasatun, madrasatin

Sukūn
d' darsun, darsī, madrasatun

Shadda
dda, ddi, ddu, ddaa, dduu, ddii, ddan, ddun, ddin, darrasa,
mudarrisun, mudarrisatun

Diphthongs
daw, day, dawrun, daysun, dayrun

All vowels
da, dā, dda, du, dā, day, dā, ddu, d', dā, daw,
dun, da, dā, din, ddi, dā, di, dda, d', dun, dā,
daw, da, dā, dā, dan, din, dun, du, day, dā, dan, dā, di, ddin, dā

Unit 1

Exercise 1

لا   لـي   لو

لى   أَلا   إلى

إي   أو

Exercise 2

ىلإ   إ   اًلِإ   الأ

Exercise 3

1 lā, lī, lū, lā, 'alā, 'ilā, 'i-ī, 'u-ū
2

Exercise 4

There are three combinations of لا in the calligraphic writing.

Unit 2

Arabic quotation

ب: 2   ت: 2   ث: 5   ن: 6   ي: 8

Exercise 1

تين   بَيْت   الثُّلاثاء

أبي   لَبن   الإِثْنَين

بابا   ليبيا   أثاث

Exercise 2

ن ا ن بْ لُ   ن ا ن ثْ إِ   ن بْ إِ

ثلُثُ   ت ا ب نَ   ل بُ لْ بُ

بِ ل ا   ا ن أ   ت يْ بَ

Exercise 3

1 tīn, 'abī, bābā, bayt, laban, lībyā, a(l)th-thulāthā', al-'ithnayn, 'athāth

2 lubnān, thuluth, bilā, 'ithnān, nabāt, 'anā, 'ibn, bulbul, bayt

Exercise 4

Food	Countries	Numbers	Family	Days	Miscellaneous
تين	لُبْنان	ثُلُث	إبْن	الإثْنَين	بِلا
لَبن	ليبيا	إثْنان	بابا	الثُّلاثاء	نَبات
			أبي		أَنا
					بُلْبُل
					بَيْت
					أثاث

Exercise 5 Relative adjectives

Lebanese: لُبْنانيّ

brown: بُنِّيّ

vegetarian: نَباتيّ

Exercise 6 Possessive pronouns

My son	إبْني
My house	بَيْتي
My father	بابا/ أبي
My daughter	بِنْتي
My door	بابي

Unit 3

Arabic quotation

م: ٦ ه: ٢ ك: ٦ ة: ١

word: كلمة

Exercise 1

لَيْمون   ثَمانِيَة   ماء

مَكَّة   كِتاب   ا لله

Exercise 2

ث م ا ن و ن   ا ل مَ نَ ا مَ ة   م ا م ا

ا ل يَ مَ ن   ا ل ك ي مْ ي ا ء   أ م ا مَ

Exercise 3

1 mā', allāh, thamāniyah, kitāb, laymūn, makkah
2 māmā, amāma, al-manāmah, al-kīmyā', thamānūn, al-yaman

Exercise 4

Food	Countries	Cities	Family	Religious	Numbers	Miscella-neous
ماء	اليَمَن	المَنامَة	ماما	الله	ثَمانون	أمامَ
لَيْمون		مَكَّة			ثَمانِيَة	الكيْمْياء
						كِتاب

238

Exercise 5

Where are you from?	مِنْ أَيْنَ أَنْتَ؟
Who are you (f.)?	مَنْ أَنْتِ؟
She is German. She is from Germany	هِيَ أَلْمانِيَّة. هِيَ مِنْ أَلْمانِيا
My mother is from Libya.	أُمِّي مِنْ لِيبْيا
He is Yemeni. He is from Yemen	هُوَ يَمَنِيّ.هُوَ مِنَ اليَمَن
Thanks be to God	الحَمْدُ لله
God the son	الله لابْن
God the father	الله لأب

Exercise 6

I am Libyan. I am from Libya	أنا مِنْ لِيبْيا. أنا لِيبِيّ
I am German. I am from Germany	أنا أَلْمانِيّ. أنا مِنْ أَلْمانِيا
Where are you (m. pl.) from?	مِنْ أَيْنَ أَنْتُمْ؟
Who are you (m.)?	مَنْ أَنْتَ؟
Are you (f.) Lebanese?	هَلْ أَنْتِ لُبْنانِيَّة؟
Is she German?	هَلْ هِيَ أَلْمانِيَّة؟
Are you (m.) Yemeni?	هَلْ أَنْتَ يَمَنِيّ؟

Exercise 7

كِتابُكُما	كِتابُكُنَّ	كِتابُكُم	كِتابُكِ	كِتابُكَ	كِتاب ←
kitābu kumā	*kitābu kunna*	*kitābu kum*	*kitābu ki*	*kitābu ka*	*kitāb*
Your book (dual)	Your book (f. pl.)	Your book (m. pl.)	Your book (f.)	Your book (m.)	Book

Exercise 8

Father of Mary	أُمُّ مَرْيَم
Mother of Mary	أَبو مَرْيَم

Unit 4

Exercise 1

ذلِك	أَكيد	هـٰذا
ذُبابَة	هـٰذِه	دين

Exercise 2

أَدَب	ذَهَب	دُبي
مَدينَة	إمام	لَذيذ

Exercise 3

1 hādhā, 'akīd, dhālik, dīn, hādhihi, dhubābah
2 dubay, dhahab, 'adab, ladhīd, 'imām, madīnah

Exercise 4

Cities	Demonstrative pronouns	Religious vocabulary	Miscellaneous
دُبي	ذلِك	إمام	لَذيذ
	هـٰذِه	دين	ذَهَب
	هـٰذا		مَدينَة
			أَدَب
			ذُبابَة
			أَكيد

Exercise 6

aubergine: باذِنْجان

240

Unit 5

Exercise 1

تذاكر	وَرْدَة	الإمارات
مَنْزِل	هَواء	دَوْلَة

Exercise 2

بَ ر ي د	يَ وْ م	ب ا رِ د
زَ يْ ت و ن	ال أُ رْ دُ ن	أ رُ ز

Exercise 3

1 al-'imārāt, wardah, tadhākir, dawlah, hawā', manzil
2 bārid, yawm, barīd, 'aruzz, al-'urdun, zaytūn

Exercise 4

Food	Countries	Public signs	Adjectives	Miscellaneous
أرُز	الأُرْدُن	بَريد	بارِد	يَوْم
زَيْتون	دَوْلَة			دَوْلَة
الإمارات	الإمارات			هَواء
				وَرْدَة
				تذاكر
				مَنْزِل

Exercise 5

admiral: أُمير ال-

hazard: الزَّهْر

bazār: بَزار

vizier: وَزير

Exercise 6

olive oil: زَيْت الزَّيْتون

Exercise 7

Trident White

Unit 6

Exercise 1

حَليب	مِلح	خُبْز
الأَحَد	مُحَمَّد	دَجاج

Exercise 2

أَحْمَر	واحِد	جَدَّة
أخ	الجَزائِر	البَحْرَيْن

Exercise 3

1 khubz, milh, halīb, dajāj, muhammad, al-'ahad
2 jaddah, wāhid, 'ahmar, al-bahrayn, al-jazā'ir, 'akh

Exercise 4

Food	Countries	Colours	Family	Numbers	Arabic names
دَجاج	البَحْرَيْن	أَحْمَر	أخ	واحِد	مُحَمَّد
خُبْز	الجَزائِر		جَدَّة		
مِلح					
حَليب					

Exercise 5

algebra: الجَبر

camel: جَمَل

alcohol: الكُحول

magazine: مَخازِن

Exercise 6

welcome: مَرْحباً

Exercise 7

جَدّة خالة حَبيبة زَوْجة

Unit 7

Exercise 1

مِشْمِش	أَسْوَد	الخَميس
السَّبْت	السّودان	مُرّاكُش

Exercise 2

سُ كَّ ر	كُ سْ كُ س	خَ مْ سَ ة
سِ تَّ ة	دِ مَ شْ ق	ت و نِ س

Exercise 3

1 al-khamīs, 'aswad, mishmish, murrākush, a(l)s-sūdān, a(l)s-sabt
2 khamsah, kuskus, sukkar, tūnis, dimashq, sittah

Exercise 4

Food	Countries and cities	Days	Numbers	Colours
كُسْكُس	تونِس	السَّبْت	سِتّة	أَسْوَد
سُكَّر	دِمَشْق	الخَمِيس	خَمْسَة	
مِشْمِش	السّودان			

Exercise 5

syrup: شَراب

assassins: حَشّاشين

artichoke: الخُرْشوف

Exercise 6

hello: السَّلامُ عَلَيْكُم (said when greeting someone any time of the day)

hello and welcome: أَهْلاً وَسَهْلا وَ مَرْحَبًا (said when welcoming someone to your home)

thank you: شُكْراً

God willing: إِنْ شاءَ الله (said when someone intends to do something in the future)

Exercise 7

دُكْتورة   سَيِّدة

Exercise 8

Hello and welcome to Kuwait.

Unit 8

Exercise 1

أَبو ظَبي   مَراحيض   شاي

الشُّرطة   الرِّباط   طَماطِم

Exercise 2

مَ ط ا ر   أَخْ ض َر   بَ ط ا ط ا

أَبْ يَ ض   خَ طَ ر   م و ر ي ط ا ن ي ا

Exercise 3

1 shāy, marāḥīd, 'abū-dhabī, ṭamāṭim, a(l)r-ribāṭ, a(l)sh-shurṭah
2 baṭāṭā, 'akhḍar, maṭār, mūrīṭānyā, khaṭar, 'abyaḍ

Exercise 4

Food	Countries and cities	Public signs	Colours
شاي	موريطانيا	مَطار	أَخْضر
طَماطِم	الرِّباط	خَطَر	أَبْيَض
بَطاطا	أَبو ظَبي	الشُّرطة	
		مَراحيض	

Exercise 5

mattress: مَطْرَح
sahara: صَحْراء
gibraltar: جَبَل طارق

Exercise 6

1 صَباحُ الخَير Good morning
2 بَعْدَ الظُّهْر afternoon
3 مَساءُ الخَير Good afternoon/evening

Exercise 7

Exercise 8

Lipton: Yellow label tea

Exercise 9

Casablanca (Spanish for White House)

Unit 9

Exercise 1

عَشَرَة	شارِع	الجُمُعَة
المَغْرِب	الأَرْبِعاء	أَرْبَعَة

Exercise 2

مَ طْ عَ م	بَ غْ د ا د	سَ بْ عَ ة
عَ بْ دُ ا ل ل ه	تِ سْ عَ ة	عُ م ا ن

Exercise 3

1 al-jumuᶜah, shāriᶜ, ᶜasharah, 'arbaᶜah, al-'arbiᶜā', al-maghrib
2 sabᶜah, baghdād, matᶜam, ᶜumān, tisᶜah, ᶜabdullāh

Exercise 4

Days	Countries	Cities	Public signs	Numbers	Arabic names
الجُمُعَة	المَغْرِب	بَغْداد	شارِع	عَشَرَةٌ	عَبْدُ الله
الأَرْبِعاء	عُمان		مَطْعَم	أَرْبَعَة	
				سَبْعَة	
				تِسْعَة	

246

Exercise 5

مَمْنوع التَّدْخين   No smoking

مَمْنوع الدُّخول   No entry

مَمْنوع وُقوف السَّيّارات   No parking

Exercise 6

عرب: العربية, عربي, مستعرب

الغرب , غربي , المغرب : غرب

Exercise 7

الأَحَد الإثْنَيْن الثُّلاثاء الأَرْبِعاء الخَميس الجُمْعَة السَّبْت

Unit 10

Exercise 1

سوق   صِفْر   أَصْفَر

قِفْ   بُرْتُقال   قَهْوَة

Exercise 2

ه ا تِ ف   أَ زْ رَ ق   فِ لَ سْ ط ي ن

فُ نْ دُ ق   سِ فا رة   إ سْ ع ا ف

Exercise 3

1 'asfar, sifr, sūq, qahwah, burtuqāl, qif
2 filast̲īn, azraq, hātif, 'isʿāf, sifārah, funduq

Exercise 4

Food	Countries	Colours	Public signs	Numbers
قَهْوَة	فِلَسْطين	أَصْفَر	سوق	صِفْر
بُرْتُقال		أَزْرَق	قِف	
			إسْعاف	
			سِفارة	
			هاتِف	
			فُنْدُق	

Exercise 5

open: مَفْتوح

closed: مَقْفول

Exercise 6

zero: صِفْر

cotton: قُطْن

giraffe: زَرافَة

sofa: صُفَّة

camera: قَمَرَة

Exercise 7

Middle East: الشَّرْقُ الأَوْسَط

the Noble Qur'an: القُرآن الكَريم

the cultural centre: المَرْكَز الثَّقافِيّ

Exercise 8

Stop: we are all against smoking

248

Unit 11

LG, Burger King, PizzaHut, Lufthansa – City Centre, Popeye,
Photocopy, Vavavoom, Seven-Up, Educational Couriers, VIP Market,
Samsung.

Credits

Illustrations in this book are the author's, except for those which are copyright free and/or licensed under a Creative Commons license, and the following, for which grateful acknowledgment is made:

Illustrations in main text: vehicle registration plates, pp. 155, 173 http://www.flickr.com/photos/woodysworld1778/; eiktub™ screenshot, p. xxiii http://www.eiktub.com/; book cover, p. 114 © 2011 Barbara Whitesides.

Back cover: © Jakub Semeniuk/iStockphoto.com, © Royalty-Free/Corbis, © agencyby/iStockphoto.com, © Andy Cook/iStockphoto.com, © Christopher Ewing/iStockphoto.com, © zebicho - Fotolia.com, © Geoffrey Holman/iStockphoto.com, © Photodisc/Getty Images, © James C. Pruitt/iStockphoto.com, © Mohamed Saber - Fotolia.com

Notes

Notes

Notes

Notes